Bodily Healing and The Atonement

Bodily Healing and The Atonement

by
Dr. T. J. McCrossan

Reedited by
Roy H. Hicks, D.D., and
Kenneth E. Hagin, D.D.

FAITH LIBRARY PUBLICATIONS

Unless otherwise indicated, Scripture quotations in this book are from the *King James Version* or are Dr. McCrossan's own literal translations from the original Greek.

Second Edition
Fourth Printing 1992

ISBN 0-89276-505-4

In the U.S. write:
Kenneth Hagin Ministries
P.O. Box 50126
Tulsa, OK 74150-0126

In Canada write:
Kenneth Hagin Ministries
P.O. Box 335
Islington (Toronto), Ontario
Canada, M9A 4X3

BOOKS BY KENNETH E. HAGIN

* Redeemed From Poverty, Sickness and Spiritual Death
* What Faith Is
* Seven Vital Steps To Receiving the Holy Spirit
* Right and Wrong Thinking
  Prayer Secrets
* Authority of the Believer (foreign only)
* How To Turn Your Faith Loose
  The Key to Scriptural Healing
  Praying To Get Results
  The Present-Day Ministry of Jesus Christ
  The Gift of Prophecy
  Healing Belongs to Us
  The Real Faith
  How You Can Know the Will of God
  Man on Three Dimensions
  The Human Spirit
  Turning Hopeless Situations Around
  Casting Your Cares Upon the Lord
  Seven Steps for Judging Prophecy
* The Interceding Christian
  Faith Food for Autumn
  Faith Food for Winter
  Faith Food for Spring
  Faith Food for Summer
* The New Birth
* Why Tongues?
* In Him
* God's Medicine
* You Can Have What You Say
  How To Write Your Own Ticket With God
* Don't Blame God
* Words
  Plead Your Case
* How To Keep Your Healing
  Laying on of Hands
  A Better Covenant
  Five Hindrances to Growth in Grace
  Why Do People Fall Under the Power?
  The Bible Way To Receive the Holy Spirit
  Godliness Is Profitable
  I Went to Hell
  Three Big Words
  Obedience in Finances
  His Name Shall Be Called Wonderful
  Paul's Revelation: The Gospel of Reconciliation
  How To Walk in Love
  The Precious Blood of Jesus
  Love Never Fails
  How God Taught Me About Prosperity
  Learning To Forget
  The Coming Restoration
  The Gifts and Calling of God
  Signs of the Times
  Learning To Flow With the Spirit of God
  The Glory of God
  Hear and Be Healed
  Knowing What Belongs to Us

Your Faith in God Will Work
* New Thresholds of Faith
* Prevailing Prayer to Peace
* Concerning Spiritual Gifts
Bible Faith Study Course
Bible Prayer Study Course
The Holy Spirit and His Gifts
* The Ministry Gifts (Study Guide)
Seven Things You Should Know About Divine Healing
El Shaddai
Zoe: The God-Kind of Life
A Commonsense Guide to Fasting
Must Christians Suffer?
The Woman Question
The Believer's Authority
Ministering to Your Family
What To Do When Faith Seems Weak and Victory Lost
Growing Up, Spiritually
Bodily Healing and the Atonement
Exceedingly Growing Faith
Understanding the Anointing
I Believe in Visions
Understanding How To Fight the Good Fight of Faith
Plans, Purposes, and Pursuits
How You Can Be Led by the Spirit of God
A Fresh Anointing
The Art of Prayer
The Price Is Not Greater Than God's Grace (Mrs. Oretha Hagin)

BOOKS BY KENNETH HAGIN JR.

* Man's Impossibility — God's Possibility
Because of Jesus
The Key to the Supernatural
* Faith Worketh by Love
Blueprint for Building Strong Faith
* Seven Hindrances to Healing
* The Past Tense of God's Word
How To Make the Dream God Gave You Come True
Faith Takes Back What the Devil's Stolen
"The Prison Door Is Open — What Are You Still Doing Inside?"
Itching Ears
Where Do We Go From Here?
How To Be a Success in Life
Get Acquainted With God
Showdown With the Devil
Unforgiveness
The Answer for Oppression
Is Your Miracle Passing You By?
Commanding Power
The Life of Obedience
Ministering to the Brokenhearted
God's Irresistible Word
Healing: Forever Settled
Don't Quit! Your Faith Will See You Through
The Untapped Power in Praise
Listen to Your Heart

*These titles are also available in Spanish. Information about other foreign translations
of several of the above titles (i.e., Finnish, French, German, Indonesian, Polish, Russian,
etc.) may be obtained by writing to: Kenneth Hagin Ministries, P.O. Box 50126, Tulsa,
Oklahoma 74150-0126.

Contents

Preface

Dr. T. J. McCrossan, noted pastor, author, Bible teacher, and highly respected Greek and Hebrew scholar, taught Greek and Hebrew languages in the Manitoba University, Manitoba, Canada, before entering the ministry.

For 18 years he was the Examiner in Greek for the Presbytery of Minneapolis, Minnesota. During this period, he not only built Bethany Presbyterian Church of that city, but for 12 years pastored the historic Oliver Presbyterian Church of Minneapolis.

It was during the revolutionary ministry of Dr. Charles S. Price that Dr. McCrossan embraced the Full Gospel message, receiving the baptism of the Holy Spirit in 1922. Thereafter, these two servants of God labored side by side in many evangelistic efforts, each complementing the other's ministry.

Roy H. Hicks

Foreword

Kenneth Hagin has stated what a great blessing this book has been to him. I echo his statement.

Not being a master of the Greek language can, at times, be a benefit. It can make one more open to the works of others who are outstanding Greek scholars.

Dr. T. J. McCrossan discovered bodily healing in the Atonement through reading his Greek New Testament. Later on he teamed up with Dr. Charles Price, embraced the Full Gospel message, and received the baptism with the Holy Spirit. He was professor of Greek and Hebrew languages at Manitoba University in Canada.

I had two highly respected men of my acquaintance, both teachers of Greek in colleges, check out the Greek and the interpretation of it by Dr. McCrossan. They both assure me it is excellent.

Reader, one of the outstanding reasons why so many of God's people are not healed is because they do not fully understand the attitude of God toward sickness. So many people waver in their faith because they have heard, expounded from the pulpit, that it is God's will for them to be sick.

May the reading of this book forever erase all doubts you may have had. May you know and confess (speak out plainly) that God took both our sins and our sickness, and placed them on our Lord Jesus, by whose stripes ye are healed.

Parts of the original work have been deleted in order to allow this to be a smaller book. Rev. Hagin and I express our heartfelt thanks to Don McCrossan, son of Dr. T. J. McCrossan, for giving permission to reprint the book.

Kay H. Hicks

Foreword

For many years I had a copy of T. J. McCrossan's book *Bodily Healing and the Atonement* published in 1930. But somehow, like good books have a way of doing, it got away from me. The amazing enlightenment it gave me into the Scriptures, however, never got away from me.

For instance, regarding the word "helpeth" in Romans 8:26: "Likewise the Spirit also helpeth our infirmities: for we know not what we should pray for as we ought: but the Spirit itself maketh intercession for us with groanings which cannot be uttered."

Dr. McCrossan brings out that this word means "take hold, together with, against." How many times the picture of the Holy Spirit taking hold together with me against the power of the enemy has put me over in prevailing prayer. As I teach others on the subject of intercessory prayer, I paint this word picture Brother McCrossan painted so clearly for me.

I like what he brings out on Romans 8:11, too. It gives me something to chew on, if you know what I mean. I teach quite often on the God-kind of "life" Jesus came to bring us (John 10:10). For that life is the enlightenment of men (John 1:4). The Greek word for this God-kind of life is *zoe*.

Dr. McCrossan shows us the work of the Holy Spirit in manifesting this *zoe* life in our physical bodies. Romans 8:11 says, "But if the Spirit of him that raised up Jesus from the dead dwell in you, he that raised up Christ from the dead shall also quicken [*zōopoiēsei*] your mortal bodies by his Spirit that dwelleth in you." He points out, "This verb 'will quicken' is *zōopoiēsei* and comes from *zoe* (life) and *poieo* (I make). It is the work of the Holy Spirit to keep making life in these mortal bodies of ours."

From an indepth study of Isaiah 53 and First Peter

2:24, Dr. McCrossan clearly proves that the original manuscripts leave no room for doubt — Christ died for our sicknesses as He died for our sins.

I am not a Hebrew or Greek scholar. But I do appreciate someone with a deep understanding of the original languages of the Bible who also has the keen insight only the Holy Spirit can give. I've known two men who especially possess these two qualities — Dr. P. C. Nelson and Dr. T. J. McCrossan.

I believe it is the will of the Lord that Dr. McCrossan's book again is available to lovers of God's Word. You see, Rev. Roy Hicks and I had often discussed its insights and lamented that we did not still possess our own copies of it. We tried to find it.

Just recently, while Brother Hicks was eating in a restaurant, he overheard people discussing *Bodily Healing and the Atonement*. He walked over to their table, excused himself, and asked if they could possibly be discussing Dr. McCrossan's book. They were. They had a copy. And they knew Dr. McCrossan's relatives, who have since given their permission to reprint this book.

I am glad to have a part in reprinting this classic. And I am especially glad to recommend it to you.

Kenneth E. Hagin

Introductory Remarks

Let us begin by asking a very important question: *"How did sickness enter this world?"*

Our answer is found in Romans 5:12, "Wherefore, as by one man sin entered into the world, and death by sin; and so death passed upon all men, for that all have sinned."

Then physical death and all that produces it are the direct results of sin.

But how came man to sin? Read Genesis 2:17 and Genesis 3:1-19, and you will find that it was Satan who caused our first parents to disobey God. Then Satan is the real originator of sin, sickness, and death.

Many deny this and say that God Himself is the real author of sickness and death because He said to Adam (Gen. 2:17), "But of the tree of the knowledge of good and evil, thou shalt not eat of it: for in the day that thou eatest thereof thou shalt surely die." But who caused Adam and Eve to disobey God's command and so bring sin, sickness, and death into this world? Satan. Then Satan, and not God, is the real author of sin, sickness, and death.

This explains why Christ said to the man whom He cured at the Pool of Bethesda (John 5:14), "Sin no more, lest a worse thing come upon thee." His sickness had come as the result of sin.

This explains also Christ's words in Mark 2:9-11, "Whether it is easier to say to the sick of the palsy, Thy sins be forgiven thee; or to say, Arise, and take up thy bed, and walk? But that ye may know that the Son of man hath power on earth to forgive sins, (he saith to the sick of the palsy,) I say unto thee, Arise, and take up thy bed, and go thy way into thine house."

The people would not believe that Christ had power to forgive this man's sins, so He says to them, in effect, "I

1

will now prove to you that I have the power to forgive sins by curing this palsy, which is one of the consequences of sin. When you see that I can cure or take away this sin-produced disease, then you will know for a certainty that I also can take away sin itself."

Again we are absolutely sure Satan is the author of sickness as well as sin, because Christ always uses the same harsh word, *epitimao,* to rebuke sickness (Satan's work) as He uses to rebuke evil spirits.

In Luke 4:35 we read, "And Jesus rebuked [*epetimēsen*] him [the evil spirit in a man], saying, Hold thy peace, and come out of him."

In Luke 4:39 we read, "And he stood over her [Simon's wife's mother], and rebuked [*epetimēsen,* the same word as in Luke 4:35] the [spirit of] fever; and it left her." Christ used the same harsh word to rebuke all sicknesses as He used to rebuke all evil spirits, because all sickness is caused by Satan. This is the only explanation.

Yes, every sickness, disease, and deformity which Christ cured while on earth was the result of sin, Satan's work. Read Acts 10:38, "How God anointed Jesus of Nazareth with the Holy Ghost and with power: who went about doing good, and healing all that were oppressed of the devil; for God was with him." Then all Christ cured, while on earth, were oppressed of the devil. This included also Lazarus' sickness, even though Christ declares (John 11:4), "This sickness is . . . for the glory of God."

Let us here examine this word "oppressed." The Greek word is *katadunasteuomenous,* the present participle passive, accusative plural of *katadunasteuo.* This comes from *kata,* down or under, and *dunasteuo,* I hold power or lordship. Then this word *katadunasteuomenous* in Acts

10:38 really means "those under the domination or lordship of Satan."

Yes, every sickness, disease, and deformity Christ
cured while on earth was the result of Satan's work, and
it is the same today.

*Not only is Satan the originator of sickness, but he is
the propagator of it, for the Bible informs us that he has
special evil spirits whose chief business is to make people
sick.*

In Luke 13:11 we read, "And, behold, there was a
woman which had a spirit of infirmity eighteen years, and
was bowed together [bent double], and could in no wise
lift up herself." Luke 13:16 informs us that this was
Satan's work: "And ought not this woman, being a
daughter of Abraham, whom Satan hath bound, lo, these
eighteen years, be loosed from this bond on the sabbath
day?"

Notice now the words "which had a spirit of infirmity." The word for "infirmity" here is *astheneia,* the commonest word in the Greek language for "sickness." Then
this poor woman had been dominated for eighteen years
by an evil spirit, *a spirit here called "a spirit of sickness."*
Yes, Satan really has "spirits of sickness" whose one great
work in this world is to propagate sickness and disease.

In Mark 9:25 we find that Satan also has "deaf and
dumb" spirits: "When Jesus saw that the people came running together, he rebuked the foul spirit, saying unto him
[Note, these evil spirits are persons.], *Thou dumb and deaf
spirit,* I charge thee, come out of him, and enter no more
into him." Then, in addition to "spirits of sickness," Satan
also has "deaf and dumb" spirits to afflict mankind.

In Mark 1:23 we read, "And there was in their

synagogue a man with an unclean [unwashed, dirty, foul] spirit." Then Satan also has spirits who are specialists in polluting men's minds and imaginations, making them immoral.

In Acts 16:16 we read of a girl who was "possessed with a spirit of divination" (literally, a spirit of Python). This was an evil spirit which gave her the ability to foretell things.

Satan, then, has all kinds of evil spirits, and thousands of these belong to that group designated as "the spirits of sickness." No wonder we read in Ephesians 6:12, "For we wrestle not against flesh and blood, but against principalities, against powers, against the rulers of the darkness of this world, against spiritual wickedness in high places."

Yes, Satan is not only the originator of sickness and disease, but he is the propagator of the same by means of these many evil spirits who obey his every command.

Division
I

Division I

Six Great Biblical Reasons Why All Christians Should Take Christ as the Healer of Their Bodies

Reason I

Because God used to heal the sick, and He is an unchangeable God.

(a) In Old Testament times, God was man's Healer.

In Exodus 15:26 we read, "If thou wilt diligently hearken to the voice of the Lord thy God, and wilt do that which is right in his sight, and wilt give ear to his commandments, and keep all his statutes, I will put none of these diseases upon thee, which I have brought upon the Egyptians: for I am the Lord that healeth thee."

In Exodus 23:25 we read, "And ye shall serve the Lord your God . . . and I will take sickness away from the midst of thee."

Psalm 103:3, "Who forgiveth all thine iniquities; who healeth all thy diseases." God is still forgiving sins, and He is still healing diseases, or else He is not the same God He used to be.

Some Bible teachers tell us the Psalmist is here only speaking of spiritual diseases. These all quote Psalm 103:4, "Who redeemeth thy life from destruction," and then say (*Modern Religion* — Healing, page 139), "Present time healing of a sick body does not redeem it from destruction, but healing the life or soul of the sin, disease, death, does redeem both body and soul from destruction, through the resurrection."

Now these friends are wrong for three reasons:

(1) Because the word for "disease" in Psalm 103:3 in the *Septuagint* is *nosos*. This word is used nine times in the *Septuagint* and twelve times in the New Testament,

7

and it always refers to physical disease.

(2) Because the word for "healeth" in Psalm 103:3 in the *Septuagint* is *iaomai*. This word is used twenty-eight times in the New Testament, and always of physical healing.

(3) Because the expression "who redeemeth" *(Septuagint)* reads *ton lutroumenon,* the one constantly redeeming (the present participle middle of *lutroō*). *The use of the present participle here teaches the blessed truth that God is now constantly employed keeping life in our bodies (keeping our hearts beating — something we have nothing whatever to do with).* We know this redemption is going on now and does not refer to the Resurrection, because of what follows in the *Septuagint*. It literally reads, "The one redeeming thy life from destruction [decay], the one crowning thee with mercy and compassion, the one satisfying thy desire with good things," etc.

The use of the present participle here, as all Greek scholars know, brings out the blessed thought that God is right now constantly doing all these things mentioned. The redemption spoken of, therefore, in Psalm 103:3 has nothing whatsoever to do with the Resurrection of the future, but tells us of something the Lord is now doing on our behalf.

Psalm 105:37, "He brought them forth also with silver and gold: and there was not one feeble person among their tribes." Why? Because God was their Healer.

Psalm 107:20, "He [God] sent [forth] his word, and healed them . . . ."

(b) In New Testament times, God was man's Healer through the Lord Jesus Christ, God in the flesh.

Matthew 9:35, "And Jesus went about all the cities and

villages, teaching . . . and preaching the gospel of the kingdom, and healing every sickness and every disease among the people." Note, Christ preached and healed publicly.

Then Mark 6:12 informs us that Christ, God in the flesh, gave power to His disciples to heal the sick. Mark 6:12,13 says, "And they [the disciples] went out, and preached that men should repent. And they cast out many devils, and anointed with oil many that were sick, and healed them." Note, these disciples, like their Lord, also held great preaching and healing campaigns.

Has God changed, or is He the very same God today that He was in Old and New Testament times?

In Malachi 3:6 we read, "For I am the Lord, I change not."

In Hebrews 13:8 we read, "Jesus Christ the same yesterday, and to day, and for ever." The Greek expression here for "the same" is *ho autos,* and means the very same identical person in every respect.

Again, James says (James 1:17), "Every good gift [including the gift of healing] . . . is from above, and cometh down from the Father of lights, with whom is no variableness, neither shadow of turning." The Greek word here for "variableness" is *parallagē.*

Here, then, James declares that God does not change even slightly. Now, God used to be:

(1) *Jehovah-shammah* — "The Lord ever present."
(2) *Jehovah-jireh* — "The Lord our provider."
(3) *Jehovah-nissi* — "The Lord our banner."
(4) *Jehovah-shalom* — "The Lord our peace."
(5) *Jehovah-raah* — "The Lord my shepherd."
(6) *Jehovah-tsidkenu* — "The Lord our righteousness."

(7) *Jehovah-rapha* — "The Lord that healeth." (Exod. 15:26)

All admit that God is still:

Jehovah-shammah — "The Lord ever present."

Jehovah-jireh — "The Lord our provider."

Jehovah-nissi — "The Lord our banner."

Jehovah-shalom — "The Lord our peace."

Jehovah-raah — "The Lord my shepherd."

Jehovah-tsidkenu — "The Lord our righteousness."

Then, beloved, He is still *Jehovah-rapha* — the Lord our Healer, for James 1:17 declares, "With [Him] is no variableness" (He does not change even slightly); or, as Hebrews 13:8 expresses it, "Jesus Christ [God] the same yesterday, and to day, and for ever."

Since God (Christ) is just the same today as in the past, we ought to expect Him to have the same healing power.

Reason II

Again, all Christians should expect God to heal their bodies today, because Christ died to atone for our sicknesses as well as for our sins.

Leading opponents of healing in the Atonement would agree on the following statements: "Did our Lord Jesus Christ by His death on the cross atone for bodily sickness and disease? No! Never!"

They would say, "The doctrine that our Lord Jesus Christ, when He died on the cross, made an atonement for the sicknesses and diseases of the body is a false doctrine, a doctrine that cannot be found from one end of the Holy Scripture to the other."

Also, "The teaching that Christ died for our diseases as He died for our sins is a human invention, and not a

Bible doctrine."

Let us now lay aside all prejudice and examine the Bible teaching on this most important subject. The writer is Scotch-Canadian, and cannot possibly believe any doctrine until he has found the best possible scriptural reasons for so doing.

(1) Isaiah is our witness to this great truth.

In Isaiah 53:4 we read, "Surely he [Christ] hath borne our griefs [*kholee,* sicknesses], and carried our sorrows [*makob,* pains]."

Kholee (sickness) is from *chalah,* to be weak, sick, or afflicted. In Deuteronomy 7:15 we read, "The Lord will take away from thee all sickness [*kholee*]." This word is translated "sickness" in Deuteronomy 28:61, First Kings 17:17, Second Kings 1:2, Second Kings 8:8, and other places.

Makob is translated "pain" in Job 33:19, "He is chastened also with pain [*makob*]." In Jeremiah 51:8 we read, "Take balm for her pain [*makob*]."

Then Isaiah 53:4 should read, "Surely he [Christ] hath borne our sicknesses, and carried our pains." Every unprejudiced Hebrew scholar must admit that this is the correct translation.

Let us now examine the verbs in Isaiah 53:4, "borne" *(nasa)* and "carried" *(sabal).*

(a) The Hebrew verb *nasa* means to bear in the sense of "suffering punishment for something." Leviticus 5:1, "And if a soul sin . . . then he shall bear [*nasa*] his iniquity." In Isaiah 53:12 we have the true meaning of *nasa* set forth: "And he [Christ] was numbered with the transgressors; and he bare [*nasa*] the sin of many."

Now how did Christ bear our sins? Vicariously, as our

Substitute. But this is the same verb used in Isaiah 53:4, "Surely he [Christ] hath borne [*nasa*] our sicknesses."

We all admit that this verb *(nasa)* in Isaiah 53:12 teaches us that Christ bore our sins vicariously; so all unprejudiced minds must admit that this very same verb *(nasa)* in Isaiah 53:4 teaches us that He (Christ) bore our sicknesses vicariously. Yes, the very same verb *(nasa)* is used of bearing our sins in Isaiah 53:12 as is used in Isaiah 53:4 of bearing our sicknesses. The clear teaching, therefore, is that Christ bore our sicknesses in the very same way that He bore our sins. There can be no other conclusion.

(b) "And carried [*sabal*] our pains." This verb *sabal* (carried) also means "to bear something as a penalty or chastisement."

Lamentations 5:7, "Our fathers have sinned . . . and we have borne [*sabal*] their iniquities." Isaiah 53:11, "He shall see of the travail of his soul, and shall be satisfied . . . for he shall bear [*sabal*] their iniquities."

Now how did Christ bear our iniquities? Vicariously, as our Substitute. Then He bore or carried our pains in the very same way, for Isaiah declares (Isa. 53:4), "Surely he hath borne [*nasa*] our sicknesses, and carried [*sabal*] our pains."

Reader, when you remember that the words in Isaiah 53:4 for "griefs" *(kholee)* and "sorrows" *(makob)* literally mean "sicknesses" and "pains"; and when you remember that the verbs of Isaiah 53:4, "borne" *(nasa)* and "carried" *(sabal)*, are the same two verbs used in Isaiah 53:12 and Isaiah 53:11 to express the tremendous fact that Christ bore vicariously our sins and our iniquities, how can you escape the logical conclusion that Christ died for our sicknesses in the very same way that He died for our sins? For all unprejudiced Hebrew scholars there is no other conclusion.

Here listen to Young's translation (page 452): "Surely our sicknesses he hath borne, and our pains he hath carried them" (Isa. 53:4). Young, the author of *Young's Concordance,* was a great Hebraist.

Listen to Dr. Isaac Leeser's translation of Isaiah 53:4: "But only our disease did he bear himself, and our pains he carried."

Again listen to Alexander McLaren, that prince of commentators (*Volume on Isaiah,* page 98): "It is to be kept in view, that the griefs, which the Servant (Christ) is here described as bearing, are literally sicknesses, and that similarly, the sorrows may be diseases. *Matthew in his quotation of this verse (Matt. 8:17) takes the words to refer to bodily ailments* — and that interpretation is part of the whole truth, for Hebrew thought drew no such sharp line of distinction between diseases of the body and those of the soul, as we are accustomed to draw. *All sickness was taken to be the consequence of sin.*

"Of these two words expressing the Servant's taking their burden on His shoulders *(nasa* and *sabal) the former implies not only the taking of it, but the bearing of it away;* and the latter emphasizes the weight of the load."

And now listen to Matthew's comment on Isaiah 53:4. Matthew 8:16,17, "When the even was come, they brought unto him many that were possessed with devils: and he cast out the spirits with his word, and healed all that were sick: That it might be fulfilled which was spoken by Esaias the prophet, saying, Himself took our infirmities, and bare our sicknesses."

Because of this 17th verse, "That it might be fulfilled [*plērōthē*, 1st Aorist passive, subjunctive, 3rd person singular of *plēroō*] which was spoken by Esaias the prophet, saying, Himself took our infirmities, and bare our sicknesses," one scholar asks: "When did our Lord bear these diseases and carry these pains? . . . It was before He came to the cross and not while He was on the cross that this prediction was fulfilled."

Of Matthew 8:17, "That it might be fulfilled [*plērōthē*] . . .," other scholars argue, "Then this prophecy of Isaiah was fulfilled in the day when our Lord Jesus Christ healed the great multitude. It was fulfilled about three years before the Lord died on the cross. The prophecy of Isaiah was fulfilled in His divine ministry of healing, and not when He hung on the cross."

Most, if not all, opponents of healing in the Atonement today declare that Matthew 8:16 was completely fulfilled before Christ died on the cross, and while He was yet alive; therefore, this prediction has nothing whatever to do with us today. It was a prediction only for the people of Christ's own day.

Let us now see a few of the awful conclusions we would be compelled to draw if this foolish and unscholarly reasoning were correct.

Matthew 12:14 tells of a meeting of the Jewish Council to destroy our Lord. The Master then quietly withdrew from the city, but great multitudes followed Him, and He healed them. Then Matthew tells us why He withdrew quietly away from these angry Pharisees.

Matthew 12:17-21, "That it might be fulfilled [*plērōthē*, the same word as in Matthew 8:17] which was spoken by Esaias the prophet, saying, Behold my servant, whom I have chosen; my beloved, in whom my soul is well pleased: I will put my spirit upon him, and he shall shew [*apaggelei*, declare] judgment to the Gentiles. He shall not strive, nor cry; neither shall any man hear his voice in the streets. A bruised reed shall he not break, and smoking flax shall he not quench, till he send forth judgment unto victory. And in his name shall the Gentiles trust."

This wonderful prediction is found in Isaiah 42:1-4. Isaiah here predicted, as Matthew asserts (Matt. 12:17): (1) That God would put His Spirit upon Christ. (2) That Christ would then declare judgment *(krisis)* to the Gentiles. (3) That Christ would be kind, patient, and loving toward the very weakest of men, for "A bruised reed shall he not break, and smoking flax shall he not quench." (4) That Christ will yet hurl forth *(ekbale)* judgment unto victory. This refers, of course, to the horrors of the Tribulation, and to the time when Christ shall come forth to destroy all His enemies and set up His kingdom. (5) "And in his name shall the Gentiles hope."

Here, then, is a great prediction from Isaiah that in the future, (1) the Gentile nations would yet hear the Gospel and find hope in Christ, and (2) that Christ would yet hurl forth judgment unto victory (referring to His coming in vengeance to destroy all His enemies); and yet — wonderful to narrate — Matthew here declares that this prophecy of Isaiah was then fulfilled, even before the Gentiles had yet heard the Gospel; and he uses the very same word to express this fulfillment that he uses in Matthew 8:17; viz., *plērōthē*, the 1st Aorist passive, subjunctive, 3rd person singular of the verb *plēroō*, I fulfill.

Matthew asserts in Matthew 12:17 that Christ did what He did on this occasion, "That it might be fulfilled

[*plērōthē*], which was spoken by Esaias the prophet," and
he here uses the very same word for "fulfilled" *(plērōthē)*
that he uses in Matthew 8:17 regarding the fulfillment of
Isaiah 53:4.

Why did Matthew declare in Matthew 12:17 that this
great prophecy of Isaiah 42:1-4 was fulfilled at this time
when it would not be fulfilled until Jesus sets up His
millennial kingdom? Because, from God's standpoint, it
was really fulfilled just as soon as Christ was here on earth,
and began His saving ministry.

But, someone asks, "Is the Aorist tense, which in-
dicates momentary completed past action, ever used to
express future events?" Yes. See Jelf's *Greek Grammar,*
Vol. 2, page 65. Here we read, "The Aorist, like the Perfect,
is also used to express future events which must certainly happen." These prophecies of Isaiah, Matthew knew,
would most assuredly be fulfilled by God, so he here uses
the Aorist tense, thus bringing out the great truth that
their fulfillment was even then assured.

Although Matthew here declares that this prediction
of Isaiah 42:1-4 had been fulfilled, who is so foolish as to
say that Christ is not still declaring judgment to the Gentiles; that He is not still patient, kind, loving, and forgiving to the very weakest of men? Has Christ yet hurled
forth *(ekbale)* judgment unto victory? No! Are all the Gentile nations yet trusting in His Name? No! Yet Matthew
asserts that this great prediction had been fulfilled just
as soon as Christ began His blessed ministry looking to
this end, and uses the very same word for "might be fulfilled" *(plērōthē)* that he employs in Matthew 8:17.

*This, then, is positive proof to every real Greek scholar
and to all unprejudiced minds that Matthew 8:16,17 is a*

prediction which will not be completely fulfilled until the end of this Church Age.

Reader, why do opponents of healing in the Atonement give one meaning to this verb *plērōthē* (might be fulfilled) in Matthew 12:17 and another meaning entirely to the very same word *(plērōthē)* in Matthew 8:17? Because the wish is father to the thought. "O consistency, thou art a jewel."

Again let us examine Luke 4:17-21, "And there was delivered unto him the book of the prophet Esaias. And when he had opened the book, he found the place where it was written, The Spirit of the Lord is upon me, because he hath anointed me to preach the gospel to the poor; he hath sent me to heal the brokenhearted, to preach deliverance to the captives, and recovering of sight to the blind, to set at liberty them that are bruised, To preach the acceptable year of the Lord."

Christ then closed the book and said, "This day is this scripture fulfilled in your ears." This prediction is found in Isaiah 61:2.

Christ did not give all of this prophecy, for Isaiah 61:2 reads, "To proclaim the acceptable year of our Lord, and the day of vengeance of our God."

Christ stopped and did not give the last part of this prediction because He had not then come in vengeance, and would not so come until after the Tribulation.

Here, then, is a wonderful prediction covering this whole Church Age. Christ is still preaching the Gospel to the poor through His disciples. He is still preaching deliverance to the captives (those bound by Satan). He is still healing the brokenhearted. He is still giving sight to the blind; and He is still setting at liberty them that are bruised, or, more literally, "them that have been enfeebled

18   T. J. McCrossan

or broken down" (the sick, *tethrausmenous*, the perfect participle passive of *thrauo*, I break down).

Although this prediction will not be completely fulfilled till Jesus comes, yet Christ declares (Luke 4:21), "This day is this scripture fulfilled in your ears." Literally this reads, "Today this Scripture has been fulfilled [*peplērōtai*] in your ears." *Peplērōtai* is the perfect passive, 3rd singular of the verb *plēroō*, I fulfill, the very same verb which we found in Matthew 8:17.

Who is foolish enough to declare, because Christ said this prophecy had been fulfilled, that therefore we need not expect His Gospel to be preached to the poor any more; and we need not expect Christ any longer to heal the blind and the brokenhearted, or deliver the enfeebled, or proclaim liberty to the captives (of Satan)? This would be nonsense.

Now the great prediction in Isaiah 53:4, "Surely he [Christ] hath borne our sicknesses and carried our pains" has been fulfilled in exactly the same way that Isaiah 42:1-4 and Isaiah 61:1,2 have been fulfilled, and it will hold good, praise God, just as long as these great prophecies hold good; viz., until Jesus comes.

And why not, since Jesus predicted (John 14:12), "He that believeth on me, the works that I do shall he do also; and greater works than these shall he do; because I go unto my Father." We should expect Christ still to perform His healing ministry or works, because He says (Matt. 28:20), " . . . lo, I am with you alway, even unto the end of the world."

We know that Christ, as the Second Person of the Blessed Trinity, is now at God's right hand. (See Acts 7:56, Romans 8:34, Ephesians 1:20, Colossians 3:1, Hebrews 1:3, and Hebrews 10:12.)

Paul has explained to us how Christ can now be at the right hand of God and at the same time be here with His Church. Second Corinthians 3:17, "Now the Lord is the Spirit" (literal translation). Again we read in Second Corinthians 3:18, "But we all . . . are changed into the same image from glory to glory, even as by the Spirit of the Lord" (literal translation). Yes, Christ is now here with His Church in the Person of the Holy Ghost, the very same Holy Ghost who worked all the miracles of Christ as recorded in Matthew 8:16.

After Christ's Ascension, He, as the Lord, by the Spirit (2 Cor. 3:17,18), continued to heal the sick for all His disciples. (See note I, Addenda Notes.)

(a) He did this for Peter. In Acts 3:16, Peter explains the cure of the man who was born lame by saying, "And his [Christ's] name through faith in his name hath made this man strong."

Again Peter says of this same wonderful cure (Acts 4:9,10, literal translation): "If we this day be examined of the good deed done to this sick man, by what means he has been cured [*sesōstai*, saved]; Be it known unto you all . . . that by the name of Jesus Christ of Nazareth, whom ye crucified . . . even by him [*touto*, by this one] does this man stand here before you whole." By here using *touto*, the dative case of the demonstrative pronoun *houtos* (the dative of instrument), Peter declares to us that this miracle was performed directly by the Lord, by the Spirit, just as all the miracles recorded in Matthew 8:16.

Remember, every miracle Christ performed while here in the flesh was performed by the power of the Spirit (Acts 10:38).

In Acts 9:34, Peter says to Aeneas, who had been in bed eight years with the palsy, "Christ Jesus heals [*iatai*] thee." Yes, Christ Jesus did all of Peter's miracles, just in the same way He did the miracles recorded in Matthew 8:16.

(b) *Again Christ, by the Holy Spirit, performed all of Paul's miracles.* Romans 15:18,19, "For I will not dare to speak of any of those things *which Christ hath not wrought by me,* to make the Gentiles obedient, by word and deed, Through mighty signs and wonders, by the power of the Spirit of God." Note, Paul here declares that the Lord Jesus Himself performed all of his (Paul's) miracles by the power of the Holy Ghost. Remember, this is the way all the miracles recorded in Matthew 8:16 were performed. See Acts 10:38.

In Acts 16:18, Paul says to the evil spirit in a woman, "I command thee in the name of Jesus Christ to come out of her." Yes, Christ, by the Holy Spirit, did all of Paul's wonderful miracles.

(c) Again we know that Christ, by the Spirit, performed all the miracles of all the disciples after Pentecost. When threatened with death, if they again preached the Gospel, the disciples went to prayer and cried to the Lord, saying (Acts 4:29,30), "And now, Lord, behold their threatenings: and grant unto thy servants, that with all boldness they may speak thy word, By thyself stretching forth the hand of thyself for physical healing [*eis iasin*]." This is an exact literal translation, and clearly proves that Jesus Christ, the Lord, by the Spirit, continued to heal the sick after Pentecost, just as He had done before He died on the cross.

Now, the Lord Jesus, by the Spirit, is just the same today. Romans 8:11, "But if the Spirit of him that raised up Jesus from the dead dwell in you, he that raised up Christ from the dead shall also quicken your mortal bodies by his Spirit dwelling in you" (present participle).

Since we have today the very same Holy Spirit dwelling in us, (1) who raised Christ from the dead, (2) who did all of Christ's miracles (Acts 10:38), (3) who did all of Paul's miracles, and all the miracles of Peter and the other disciples, why not expect this same Jesus, the Lord, by the Spirit, to continue His miraculous work?

Just here let us quote the words of Delitzsch in his wonderful exposition of Isaiah 53:4. Delitzsch was, without exception, the greatest Hebrew scholar in Germany. He taught Hebrew at Rostock, Erlangen, and Leipzig. As a Hebraist there is no opponent of healing in the Atonement today who can begin to compare with Delitzsch. Besides being the greatest of all Hebraists, he was also a deeply spiritual man.

Regarding Isaiah 53:4, Delitzsch says, "Freely but faithfully does the Gospel of Matthew translate this text, 'Himself took our infirmities and carried our sicknesses.' The help which Jesus rendered in all kinds of bodily sickness is taken in Matthew to be a fulfillment of what in Isaiah is prophesied of the Servant of Jehovah. The Hebrew verbs of the text, when used of sin, signify to assume as a heavy burden and bear away the guilt of sin, as one's own; that is, to bear sin mediatorially in order to atone for it. But here, where not our sins, but our sicknesses and pains are the object, the mediatorial sense remains the same.

"It is not meant that the Servant of Jehovah merely entered into the fellowship of our sufferings, but that He took upon Himself the sufferings that we had to bear, and deserved to bear; and, therefore, He not only bore them away, but also in His own person endured them in order to discharge us from them. Now when one takes sufferings upon himself which another had to bear, and does this, not merely in fellowship with him, but in his stead, we call it Substitution."

Here, then, Delitzsch, perhaps the greatest of all modern Hebraists, declares that the bearing and removing of our sicknesses and pains — so clearly taught in Isaiah 53:4 — is an integral part of Christ's redeeming work; or, in other words, that bodily healing is in the Atonement. This agrees with the findings of Young, Leeser, and McLaren already quoted.

The same two verbs "borne" *(nasa)* and "carried" *(sabal)* of Isaiah 53:4 — where we are told, "Christ bore our sicknesses and carried our pains" — are the very same two verbs used in Isaiah 53:11,12 to express the great truth that Christ bore vicariously our sins and our iniquities.

In the face of such a stupendous fact, how utterly unscholarly to say that healing in the Atonement is an unscriptural doctrine; "a mere human invention."

Let us here again quote Matthew 8:16,17, "When the even was come, they brought unto him many that were possessed with devils: and he cast out the spirits with his word, and healed all that were sick: That it might be fulfilled which was spoken by Esaias the prophet, saying, Himself took our infirmities, and bare our sicknesses."

Again we are absolutely sure this prediction is for this Church Age, because of this word "our" in both Isaiah 53:4 and 5. In Isaiah 53:4 we read, "Surely he hath borne vicariously [*nasa*] our sicknesses, and carried vicariously [*sabal*] our pains." In verse 5 we read, "He was wounded for our transgressions, he was bruised for our iniquities."

The word for "our" in Isaiah 53:5 (referring to our sins) is expressed in the Hebrew by the same suffix that expresses this same word in Isaiah 53:4, where it refers to our sicknesses. It therefore refers to the very same persons, and we challenge any Hebrew scholar to prove otherwise. Since we are included in the "our" of Isaiah 53:5, "He was wounded for our transgressions," we also must be included in the "our" of Isaiah 53:4, "Surely he hath borne our sicknesses and carried our pains."

Again we are very sure that the "our" of Isaiah 53:4 and Matthew 8:17 includes us today, because of the way Matthew expresses himself in the Greek: "Himself took our infirmities." "Our infirmities" reads in Greek, *tas astheneias hēmōn* (the sicknesses of us).

Turn now to First Corinthians 15:3 and you read, "Christ died for our sins." "For our sins" reads in the Greek *uper tōn hamartiōn hēmōn* (for the sins of us). In First Peter 2:24, the same word for "our" *(hēmōn)* is used: "Who his own self bare our sins in his own body on the tree." "Our sins" here reads in the Greek *tas hamartias hēmōn* (the sins of us). John gives us the same blessed truth in First John 4:10, ". . . and sent his Son to be the propitiation for our sins." "For our sins" reads in the Greek *peri tōn hamartiōn hēmōn* (for the sins of us).

Now since Matthew declares (Matt. 8:17), "Himself [Christ] took our infirmities [the infirmities of us], and bare our sicknesses [the sicknesses of us]," and uses the very same word for "us" *(hēmōn)* that Paul, Peter and John employ when telling us that Christ died for our sins; viz., *hēmōn, we can only conclude that the use of the same*

*Greek word for "us" (hēmōn) in Matthew 8:17, First Cor-
inthians 15:3, First Peter 2:24, and First John 4:10 must
mean that Christ took the infirmities and sicknesses of the
very same persons for whose sins He died.* Any other conclusion is most unscholarly and gives a false meaning entirely to the Greek text. Greek is such an exact language
that if different persons were here meant, this fact would
most assuredly have been indicated by some word or
phrase of differentiation.

*Trying to make Isaiah 53:4 and Matthew 8:17 refer only
to the people of Christ's own day and not to us is just as
absurd and unscholarly as trying to persuade us that the
Book of James is not for this Church Age, but only for the
twelve scattered tribes, or the Jews of the Tribulation
period.* We shall reveal the utter nonsense of this teaching
later.

To substantiate our conclusions from Isaiah 53:4 and
Matthew 8:17, let us here quote the words of three great
Spirit-filled Bible scholars.

(a) A. J. Gordon (*Ministry of Healing*, pages 16,17),
"The yoke of His cross by which He lifted our iniquities,
took hold also of our diseases; — He who entered into
mysterious sympathy with our pain — which is the fruit
of sin — also put Himself underneath our pain, which is
the penalty of sin. In other words the passage seems to
teach that Christ endured vicariously our diseases, as well
as our iniquities." This agrees exactly with the conclusion
of Delitzsch, the great Hebraist.

(b) Listen to Andrew Murray (*Divine Healing*, pages
99 and 119): "It is not said only that the Lord's righteous
Servant had borne our sins, but also that He has borne
our sicknesses. Thus His bearing our sicknesses forms an

integral part of the Redeemer's work, as well as bearing
our sins. — The body and the soul have been created to
serve together as a habitation of God: the sickly condition of the body is — as well as that of the soul — a consequence of sin, and that is what Jesus is come to bear, to
expiate and to conquer."

(c) Listen also to A. B. Simpson (*The Gospel of Healing,* page 17): "Therefore as He hath borne our sins, Jesus
Christ has also borne away, and carried off our sicknesses;
yea, and even our pains, so that abiding in Him, we may
be fully delivered from both sickness and pain. Thus by
His stripes we are healed. Blessed and glorious
Burden-Bearer."

(2) Again Peter is our witness to this great fact that
bodily healing is in the Atonement.

In First Peter 2:24 we read the blessed words, "Who
his own self bare our sins in his own body on the tree . . .
by whose stripes [*molopi,* bruise] ye were healed."

Peter here states (1) that Christ bore our sins on the
cross, and (2) that by His stripes (literally bruise) ye were
healed.

This agrees exactly with Isaiah 53:5, which reads in
the *Septuagint* (Greek version of the Old Testament), "But
he was wounded on account of our sins, and was bruised
because of our iniquities: the chastisement of our peace
was upon him; and by his bruise [*to molopi autou,* by the
bruise of Him] we are healed."

Here note two facts: (1) That the word for "healed"
here, both in the *Septuagint* and the Greek New Testament, is *iaomai, a verb that always speaks of physical healing in the New Testament.* It is used 28 times in the New
Testament, and always in connection with physical heal-

ing. The Greek word for "physician" is *iatros,* a noun
derived from this same verb *iaomai.* We can, therefore, be
fully assured that when Peter declares, "By ... [His]
stripes [bruise] ye were healed," he is referring to our bodily
healing, and not to any spiritual healing. (2) Note second-
ly here that both Isaiah and Peter use the singular word
"bruise" or "stripe" *(molopi)* and not "bruises" or
"stripes." Why?

In Matthew 27:26 we read regarding Pilate, ". . . and
when he had scourged Jesus, he delivered him to be
crucified." This literally reads, "and having scourged
Jesus, he delivered him to be crucified." Mark 15:15 gives
us the same information.

*Now why do Isaiah (in the Septuagint) and Peter use
the word molopi (dative singular of molops), and not molopsi (bruises, dative plural)?*

The word *molops* means "the mark of a blow" or "a
bruise." If Christ had been so scourged that the mark of
each blow could plainly have been seen on His back, then
the rule of Greek grammar would have demanded here the
use of *molopsi* (bruises), and not the singular *molopi*
(bruise).

The use of the dative singular here, *molopi* (the dative
of instrument), tells us, as clearly as language can express
it, that our dear Savior's back had been so terribly
scourged that no one blow could possibly be distinguished
from the other. Every spot on His back was so bruised
and lacerated that it was just like one great bruise. *Had
there been one quarter inch of space between any two of
the bruises, the Greek here must then have read molopsi
(bruises) and not molopi (bruise).*

The Jews had a law that no person should be given

more than 40 stripes when flogged, but the Romans had no such law, so they often scourged their victim until he bled to death.

But besides scourging Christ on the back until His whole back was just one great bruise, the cruel Romans plucked out His whiskers by the roots and spat upon Him. Read Isaiah 50:6, "I gave my back to the smiters, and my cheeks to them that plucked off the hair: I hid not my face from shame and spitting."

Just here let us quote from Geikie's *Life of Christ*, as he describes Christ's scourging: "Victims condemned to the cross first underwent the hideous torture of the scourge, and this was immediately inflicted on Jesus. He was now seized by some of the soldiers standing near, and after being stripped to the waist, was bound in a stooping posture, His hands being behind His back, to a post, or a block, near the tribunal. He was then beaten at the pleasure of the soldiers, with knots of rope, or plaited leathern thongs, armed at the ends with acorn shaped drops of lead, or small sharp pointed bones. In many cases not only was the back of the person scourged cut open in all directions, but even the eyes, the face, and the breast were torn, and teeth not seldom knocked out. Under the fury of the countless stripes, the victims sometimes sank — amidst screams, convulsive leaps, and distortions — into a senseless heap; sometimes died on the spot; sometimes were taken away, an unrecognizable mass of bleeding flesh, to find deliverance in death, from the inflammation and fever, sickness and shame.

"The scourging of Jesus was of the severest, for the soldiers only too gladly vented on any Jew the grudge they bore that nation, and they would, doubtless, try if they could not force out the confession which His silence had denied to the governor. Besides, He was to be crucified, and the harder the scourging, the less life there would be left to detain them afterwards on guard at the cross."

Eusebius, the Early Church historian, describes a Roman scourging of some martyrs thus: "All around were horrified to see them so torn with the scourges that their very veins were laid bare, and the inner muscles and sinews, and even their very bowels were exposed."

On Christ's poor, bruised back they now laid the heavy cross (John 9:17).

Reader, now you understand why Peter asserts with Isaiah, that "by his bruise [not bruises], ye were healed," referring, as we have clearly proven from the use of this verb "healed" *(iaomai),* to bodily healing. Much of His precious blood was doubtless shed while receiving that awful bruise for our physical healing, but the rest of His precious blood was reserved to be shed on the cross for our sins.

Yes, Peter here (1 Peter 2:24) clearly teaches that Christ not only suffered, bled, and died for our sins, but also for our physical healing.

(3) Again Paul, as well as Isaiah and Peter, is our witness to this same great fact that bodily healing is in the Atonement.

In First Corinthians 6:19 Paul says, "What! know ye not that your body is the temple of the Holy Ghost which is in you, which ye have of God, and ye are not your own? For ye are bought [*ēgorasthēte*] with a price: therefore glorify God in your body, and in your spirit, which are God's." Note, our body is God's as well as our spirit.

The Greek construction here reads *hatina estin tou*

theou (which are of the God). *Hatina* is the nominative plural, neuter of the relative pronoun *hostis*, and so includes both body and spirit. *Theou* is the genitive singular of *theos* (God), the genitive of source or origin, and so brings out the gracious truth that our bodies are God's for the very same reason that our spirits are His; viz., because both originated from Him. This being true, we are not surprised here to read that both have been bought with a price. *What was the price paid to thus purchase our body and our spirit? The blood of the Lord Jesus Christ. How* can we be absolutely certain of this?

The word for "bought" here gives us the clue. This word is *ēgorasthēte*, the 1st Aorist passive, 2nd plural of *agorazō*, I buy or redeem. Turn now to Revelation 5:9, "And they sung a new song, saying, Thou art worthy to take the book, and to open the seals thereof: for thou wast slain, and hast redeemed [*ēgorasas*] us to God by thy blood."

The word "redeemed" here is *ēgorasas*, the 1st Aorist, 2nd person singular of *agorazō*, I buy, the very same word that Paul uses in First Corinthians 6:20, where he asserts that both our body and spirit were bought or redeemed with a price. Peter also uses this same word *(agorazō)* to express Christ's redemptive work (2 Peter 2:1).

Now John asserts (Rev. 5:9) that Christ redeemed us to God (or bought us) with His blood. Paul asserts (1 Cor. 6:19,20) that the "us" of Revelation 5:9 includes our bodies as well as our spirits, and uses the very same word for "bought" or "redeemed" that John uses.

Then these two passages together teach most clearly the blessed truth that, when Christ shed His blood at the awful scourging and on the cross, He redeemed both our

bodies and our spirits by His blood, the price paid. No un-
prejudiced Greek scholar can possibly draw any other con-
clusion as he closely studies First Corinthians 6:19,20 and
Revelation 5:9. Yes, praise God, Paul clearly teaches in
First Corinthians 6:19,20 that bodily healing is in the
Atonement.

"But," someone says, "if Paul here teaches that Christ
died to redeem our body as well as our soul, why does he
say in Romans 8:23, '. . . we ourselves groan within
ourselves, waiting for the adoption, . . . the redemption of
our body'? Does not Paul here teach that our body has
not yet been redeemed?"

See Scofield's Bible note on Romans 3:24. He here
shows the meaning of the three verbs in the New Testament translated "redeemed"; viz., *agorazo, exagorazo,* and
lutroo.

In Romans 8:23, Paul uses the word *apolutrōsis.* This
is derived from *apo,* from, and *lutroo,* "I set free after a
ransom has been paid." Then *apolutrōsis* (redemption) in
Romans 8:23 means "a setting free of what has been
already ransomed."

In First Corinthians 6:19,20 Paul declares we have now
been "redeemed" *(agorazo),* body and spirit, by having the
price paid for us. In Galatians 3:13 he asserts we have been
"redeemed," or "bought out from under" *(exagorazo)* the
curse of law; but, as yet, we have not experienced "redemption" *(apolutrōsis,* Rom. 8:23) in the sense that we are now
entirely freed from all the evil results of our former bondage to Satan. Our bodies are still subject to pain, sickness,
and death, and will be until we receive our glorified bodies
— the redemption which Paul calls *apolutrōsis* (Rom. 8:23).

Remember Paul here asserts (1 Cor. 6:20) that we have

been bought, body and spirit, with a price, and uses the very same verb for "bought" *(agorazo)* as is translated "redeemed" in Revelation 5:9, where we are told the price paid was "the blood of Christ."

Note, Paul uses the Aorist tense of this verb in First Corinthians 6:20; viz., *ēgorasthēte*, which tells us, as plainly as words can express it, that the redemption of spirit and body was then something already accomplished.

But, although the price of our redemption already had been paid, Paul says in Ephesians 4:30, "And grieve not the Holy Spirit of God by which ye have been sealed [literal reading] unto the day of redemption [*apolutrōsis* of Rom. 8:23]." This is positive proof, therefore, that this "redemption" of Romans 8:23 *(apolutrōsis)* refers to something which takes place subsequent to that redemption which saves our souls, when we accept Christ as our Savior, as the One who shed His blood to redeem us body and soul.

Our spirits also, like our bodies, are still awaiting this same "redemption" (apolutrōsis), for Paul says (Rom. 8:23, ". . . we ourselves [*hemeis autoi*] groan within ourselves." "We ourselves" here refers to our spirits, which inhabit and control our bodies. We are absolutely sure of this, because the pronoun "we" *(hemeis)* is the very same word that we find in Revelation 1:5, ". . . and washed us [*hemas*, Accusative of *hemeis*] from our sins in his own blood." Then our redeemed spirits, which have been washed from sin, as well as our redeemed bodies, can now groan and suffer pain. The word "groan" *(stenazo)* means to sigh deeply, or moan with pain and anguish, whether mental or physical.

Yes, our spirits, as well as our bodies, can now suffer sorrow, pain, and anguish.

All will be changed, however, when this redemption, called *apolutrōsis* (the setting free from), takes place. When this "redemption," *apolutrōsis* (Rom. 8:23), does take place, then both our spirits and our bodies will be completely free from sorrow, pain, weeping, and all the consequences of the sin bondage from which Christ has already redeemed us by His awful scourging and death. See Revelation 21:4. (See note II, Addenda Notes.)

Again Paul teaches this same great truth, that Christ died for our sicknesses as well as for our sins, in Galatians 3:13, "Christ hath redeemed us from the curse of the law, being made a curse for us."

The Greek word here for "redeem" is not *agorazo*, but *exagorazo*, and means "to purchase or redeem out from or away from." The word for "curse" here is *katara*. Note this word.

Turn now to Deuteronomy 28:15-47, and you will find that every kind of sickness and disease is included in the curse of the law. In Deuteronomy 28:1 we read, "And it shall come to pass, if thou shalt hearken diligently unto the voice of the Lord thy God, to observe and to do all his commandments which I command thee this day, that the Lord thy God will set thee on high above all the nations of the earth." Verses 2 to 14 then set forth the wonderful blessings of God, if only they will obey His commands.

Now read Deuteronomy 28:15,21,22,27,28, "But it shall come to pass, if thou wilt not hearken unto the voice of the Lord thy God, to observe to do all his commandments and his statutes which I command thee this day; that all these curses [*katarai*] shall come upon thee, and overtake thee . . . The Lord shall make the pestilence cleave unto thee ... The Lord shall smite thee with a consumption, and with a fever, and with an inflammation ... with the botch of Egypt, and with emerods, and with the scab, and with the itch ... The Lord shall smite thee with madness, and blindness, and astonishment of heart ...."

Remember that Deuteronomy 28:15 calls all these sicknesses which would follow disobedience to God's law, "curses" *(katarai* in the *Septuagint)*. Now this is the nominative plural of the very word Paul uses when he says (Gal. 3:13), "Christ hath redeemed us from the curse [*katara*] of the law, being made [*genomenos*, having become] a curse [*katara*] for us."

Since sickness was one of the curses *(katara)* of the law, and Christ died to redeem us from the curse *(katara)* of the law, by becoming a curse *(katara)* for us (substitutionary Atonement); therefore, according to Paul's teaching, bodily healing is in the Atonement. In the light of Isaiah 53:4 and Isaiah 53:11 and 12, this is what we would expect Paul to teach.

(4) Again we know that healing is in the Atonement because of certain types found in the Old Testament.

(a) The cleansing of the leper.

In Leviticus 14:1-7 we find that when God desired to cleanse a leper, He commanded the priest to take two birds alive. He killed one of these birds over running water and caught its blood in an earthen vessel. The live bird was dipped into the blood of the slain bird. After the priest sprinkled the poor leper seven times with the blood of the dead bird, he set the live bird, which had been dipped into the blood of the dead bird, free, and it flew away toward heaven.

This most assuredly was a type of bodily cleansing and

healing through the death and resurrection of our Lord. The dead bird was a type of the crucified Christ; the live bird a type of the resurrected Christ. No other explanation seems adequate.

(b) Another type of bodily healing in the Atonement is found in the Passover lamb.

In Exodus 12:7,13, we read, "And they shall take of the blood, and strike it on the two side posts and on the upper door posts of the houses . . . and when I see the blood, I will pass over you."

But what did they do with the flesh of that slain lamb on that sacred occasion?

Exodus 12:8 informs us, "And they shall eat the flesh in that night, roast with fire, and unleavened bread."

The blood, then, was to be sprinkled on the door posts to save them from the wrath of God, but the flesh of that first Passover lamb was to be eaten for their physical benefits.

Read now First Corinthians 5:7, "For even Christ our passover is sacrificed for us." Then the Passover lamb was a type of the crucified Christ, the Lamb of God.

Since Christ is our Passover lamb, we must conclude: (1) That His blood — like the blood of the Passover lamb — was shed to save us from the wrath of God; and (2) that His flesh — like the flesh of the first Passover lamb — was broken for our physical benefits; or, as Peter puts it, (1 Peter 2:24) ". . . by the bruise of whom ye were healed [healed physically, *iaomai*]."

In Numbers 9:12 we read that not one single bone of the Passover lamb could be broken, and John 19:36 informs us that, because of this prediction, not one of Christ's bones was broken.

Reader, when God was so particular that Christ, our Passover lamb, should thus fulfill "type" in the minutest detail, and since the flesh of every Passover lamb was always used to bless men physically, have we not a perfect right to conclude (as First Peter 2:24 clearly asserts), that the flesh of Christ, our Passover lamb, was broken for our physical benefits, and that bodily healing therefore is in the Atonement?

Reason III

Again, all saints should expect God to heal their sicknesses today, because all sickness is the result of Satan's work, when he introduced sin into this world, and Christ was manifested to destroy Satan's work.

Acts 10:38 proves to us conclusively that all the diseases Christ cured while on earth had been caused by Satan. Acts 10:38, "God anointed Jesus of Nazareth with the Holy Ghost and with power: who went about doing good, and healing all that were oppressed of the devil; for God was with him."

The word here for "oppressed" is *katadunasteuomenous,* the present participle, passive of *katadunasteuo,* I dominate or exercise lordship over.

Then all whom Christ healed while on earth were diseased or afflicted because Satan had gotten the lordship, either over them or their ancestors. Yes, every physical ill Christ cured, Peter here assures us, was the result of Satan's work.

But Jesus came, died on the cross, and rose again that He might destroy the works of the devil.

Hebrews 2:14, "Forasmuch then as the children are partakers of flesh and blood, he also himself likewise took part of the same; that through death he might destroy him that had the power of death, that is, the devil." Then Christ died to destroy Satan's power over death. Is not sickness one method by which Satan causes death? Then Christ died to destroy (annul the power of) sickness.

John reveals the same truth in First John 3:8, "For this purpose the Son of God was manifested, that he might destroy the works of the devil." Is sickness the result of the devil's work? Yes! Then Christ died and rose again to destroy (annul the power of) sickness.

Reason IV

A fourth reason why all Christians should expect God to heal their sick bodies today is because the very same Holy Spirit who did all of Christ's miracles and raised Him from the dead is still in the Church, and has all His old-time, life-giving power.

In John 14:16, Christ declares emphatically that the Holy Ghost would abide with us forever. Then, in First Thessalonians 1:5, Paul asserts, "For our gospel came not unto you in word only, but also in power [*dunamis*], and in the Holy Ghost." Now this word for "power" *(dunamis)* is the Holy Ghost power of Luke 24:49 and Acts 1:8. Again Paul declares (2 Tim. 1:7), "For God hath not given us [the members of His true Church] the spirit of fear; but of power [*dunamis*, Holy Ghost power] . . . ."

Then the Holy Ghost, who is now abiding in us, is the Holy Ghost with power *(dunamis)*, the very same Holy Ghost who controlled all of Christ's actions while on earth. Luke 4:14, "And Jesus returned in the power [*dunamis*] of the Spirit into Galilee." This same Holy Spirit, who is now in the Church, was He who anointed Christ and gave

Him the power to work all His miracles. Acts 10:38, "God anointed Jesus of Nazareth with the Holy Ghost and with power [*dunamis*]: who went about doing good, and healing all that were oppressed of the devil." Remember, Christ did all His miracles in the power of the Holy Ghost, and not in His own power as the Second Person of the Blessed Trinity.

Reader, Christ has assured us that this same Holy Ghost power, called *dunamis,* is for each of His saints today. Acts 1:8, "But ye shall receive power [*dunamis*] after that the Holy Ghost is come upon you."

Paul, too, has assured us in Second Timothy 1:7 and elsewhere that God has given to His Church "the Holy Spirit of power" *(dunamis),* the very same Holy Spirit who controlled Christ's life (Luke 4:14) and wrought all His miracles (Acts 10:38), and the very same Holy Spirit who worked all of Paul's miracles. Romans 15:18,19, "For I will not dare to speak of any of those things which Christ hath not wrought by me . . . Through mighty signs and wonders, by the power [*dunamis*] of the Spirit of God."

Since the very same Holy Spirit who did all of Christ's miracles and all of Paul's miracles is in the Church today with all His old-time power (dunamis), why should we not expect Him to heal the sick today?

No wonder Paul declares (Rom. 8:26), "The Spirit also helpeth our infirmities [*astheneiais*]." This Greek word *astheneiais* is the dative plural of *astheneia,* the commonest word in the Greek language for "sickness." But note well the word here translated "helpeth" *(sunantilambanetai).* This is the present tense, 3rd person singular of the deponent verb *sunantilambanomai,* and comes from *sun,* together with; *anti,* against; and *lambano,* I take hold of. This word, therefore, means "to take hold against together with."

Thus, in Romans 8:26 we are told that the Holy Ghost takes hold against our sicknesses together with someone. With whom? Why, with ourselves, whenever we meet the needful conditions, the conditions set forth in John 15:7, "If ye abide in me, and my words abide in you, ye shall ask what ye will, and it shall be done unto you."

Yes, Romans 8:26 teaches us that it is just as much the work of the Holy Spirit today "to take hold against our sicknesses" as it is to convict sinners of their sin.

Listen now to Romans 8:11, "But if the Spirit of him that raised up Jesus from the dead dwell in you, he that raised up Christ from the dead shall also quicken [*zōopoiēsei*] your mortal [*thnēta*] bodies by his Spirit that dwelleth in you."

This verb "will quicken" is *zōopoiēsei*, the future, 3rd person singular of *zōopoieō*, and comes from *zōē*, life, and *poieō*, I make.

Dr. Gaebelein (*The Healing Question*, page 78) says of this verse (Rom. 8:11), "The quickening of the believer's body is not a present fact, but awaits future realization. The word 'quicken' means to make alive that which is dead. The quickening takes place in resurrection, when the believer's body will be made like unto His own glorious body."

Dr. Gaebelein says, "The word 'quicken' here means to make alive that which is dead." This is true when this word is used with *nekrous*, as in Romans 4:17, ". . . even God who quickeneth the dead." "Quickeneth" here is *zōopoiountos*, the present participle, genitive, masculine of *zōopoieō*, and so literally reads, "God giving life to or quickening the dead *(nekrous)." Nekrous* is the accusative plural of *nekros,* a dead human body.

The writer has studied closely a great many Greek authors, but never has he found a single instance where the word *thnētos* means a dead body. *Thnētos* (mortal) is an adjective derived from *thnēskō,* I died, and always means "liable to, or subject to death," in contrast with *athanatos,* immortal. The Greek word for a dead human body is *nekros,* but never *thnētos,* which always refers to something "subject to death," but never, never to a dead body.

Let Paul explain what he means by the word *thnētos,* mortal. Romans 6:12, "Let not sin reign in your mortal [*thnētos,* the same word as in Romans 8:11] body," etc. Had Paul said, "Let not sin reign in your dead body," it would have been utter nonsense.

Again Paul gives us the true meaning of *thnētos* in Second Corinthians 4:11, "For we which live are always delivered unto death for Jesus' sake, that the life also of Jesus might be made manifest in our mortal flesh." If "our mortal [*thnētos*] flesh" here meant "our dead flesh," how could we, after our bodies were dead, manifest forth the life of Christ? No! We are now to manifest forth the life of Jesus Christ in these bodies which are subject to death, for the word "mortal" *(thnētos)* never, never means a dead body, but always something which is subject to death, but not yet dead.

John Calvin, that superb Greek scholar, is therefore correct when he says of Romans 8:11, "The quickening of the mortal body here cannot refer to the resurrection of the saints, but must mean a giving of life to their bodies, while here upon earth, through the Spirit." No real Greek scholar — one skilled in Greek grammar — can possibly come to any other conclusion.

Let us now read again Romans 8:11, "If the Spirit of him that raised up Jesus from the dead dwell in you, he that raised up Christ from the dead shall also quicken your mortal bodies [these bodies subject to death, but not dead] by his Spirit that dwelleth in you."

The word for "quicken" here is *zōopoiēsei*. This word comes from *zōē*, life, and *poieō*, I make. Then it is the work of the Spirit "to make life." Second Corinthians 3:6 says, " . . . for the letter killeth, but the spirit giveth life [*zōopoiei*]."

Since it is the work of the Holy Spirit, as Paul assures us, to keep making life in these mortal bodies of ours, no wonder this apostle asserts (Rom. 8:26), "The Spirit takes hold against our sicknesses together with."

This verse proves that, while it is the work of the Spirit to keep making life in our mortal bodies (bodies subject to sickness and death), yet He will not do this blessed work unless we, God's saints, do our part, and take hold together with Him.

What is our part? John 15:7 gives the explanation, "If ye abide in me, and my words abide in you, ye shall ask what ye will, and it shall be done unto you." In other words, we must let the Holy Spirit control us in thought, word, and deed, and then He "will take hold against our sicknesses together with" ourselves (literal reading of Romans 8:26). The result will be that He (the Holy Spirit) will keep making life (the exact meaning of *zōopoieō)* in these mortal bodies of ours.

Yes, praise God, all Christians should expect God to heal their bodies today, because the very same Holy Spirit who did all of Christ's miracles (Acts 10:38) and all of Paul's miracles (Rom. 15:19) is still in the Church as "the maker of life" *(zōopoieō)*, and He is here "to take hold against our sicknesses together with" ourselves, as Romans 8:26 asserts. HALLELUJAH!

Reason V

Again, all Christians should believe in divine healing today because of: (a) Christ's last Great Commission, and (b) God's direct command in James 5:14.

(a) Examine here Christ's last Commission to His disciples in Mark 16:17,18: "And these signs shall follow them that believe [literally "to those believing"]; In my name shall they cast out devils; they shall speak with new tongues; They shall take up serpents [as Paul did, Acts 28:3-5]; and if they drink any deadly thing, it shall not hurt them; *they shall lay hands on the sick, and they shall recover.*"

Here, then, is a direct command from Christ that His followers should pray for the sick and expect Him to heal them.

A few scholars have denied the authenticity of these verses in Mark 16, but Irenaeus quotes these verses as a part of Mark's Gospel, and, remember, he was a pupil of Polycarp, who in turn was a pupil of John the Apostle. This is positive proof that these words are genuine. (See Morrison's *Commentary on Mark* for a full discussion on this suject.)

(b) Here listen to James 5:14,15, "Is any sick among you? let him call for the elders of the church; and let them pray over him, anointing him with oil in the name of the Lord: And the prayer of faith shall save the sick, and the

Lord shall raise him up."

The word "call" here is *proskalesasthō*, the 1st Aorist,
imperative, middle, 3rd singular of *proskaleō*, I call or summon. It is therefore a direct command from God, a command that most saints have never yet obeyed. But look
at God's promise, if only we will obey this command.
James 5:15, "The prayer of faith shall save the sick, and
the Lord shall raise him up; and if he have committed sins,
they shall be forgiven him." *Is this a part of God's Word?
Yes. Then, let us obey it and see how marvelously God
fulfills His promises.*

One opponent of divine healing quotes James 5:14,15
and then says, "Note that James says, 'save' not cure or
heal. Now this word 'save' would certainly lead us to
believe that James was speaking about sin and the sin sick
soul, rather than bodily sickness."

We know James was here speaking of physical sickness
because:

(1) The word for "save" here is *sōsei*, the future, 3rd
singular of *sōzō*, the very word used by Christ every time
He said to a sick person, "Thy faith hath made thee
whole." See Matthew 9:22, Mark 6:56, Mark 10:52, Luke
8:48, Luke 17:19, etc.

(2) Because of the word James uses for "the sick," as
in the Scripture "the prayer of faith shall save the sick"
(ton kamnonta). Kamnonta is the present participle,
masculine accusative of *kamno,* to be tired, exhausted,
sick, or ill, and literally reads, "the one being sick or exhausted." This is the word used to express Job's physical
sickness. See *Septuagint* (Job 17:2).

(3) Again the word "raise" *(egerei)* here speaks of
physical illness. It is the future of *egeiro,* I raise or lift

up, the very word used in Mark 1:31, where Christ "lifted up" Simon's mother-in-law, who was sick of a fever.

(4) Again we are absolutely sure that this sickness of James 5:14 refers to physical sickness and not spiritual, because this epistle was written to Church saints. James 1:19 speaks of "my beloved brethren," words which always and only refer to Church saints. See Division III, where we prove most conclusively that James wrote his epistle to Church saints. This being so, then their sins already were forgiven — they were saved. But if he (the sick one) may have committed (the subjunctive mood with the perfect participle) sins, they shall be forgiven him, James declares. If James had been here writing to a people who were spiritually sick or unsaved, would he have used the subjunctive mood, and said, "And if he may have committed sins"? Never. If they had been spiritually sick or unsaved, there would have been no "if" about it; they would all have needed forgiveness.

For these four reasons we are absolutely sure James 5:14,15 is God's command to His physically sick saints, a command, however, which comparatively few obey.

But what is here meant by "the prayer of faith shall save the sick" (James 5:15)? Many say it refers only to the faith of the elders who offer the prayer, and not to the faith of the sick persons. This is not correct, for Mark 9:17-27 tells us of a poor father who brought his demon-possessed son to the Lord and said, "If thou canst do any thing, have compassion on us, and help us." Jesus replied, "If thou canst believe, all things are possible to him that believeth [to him believing]."

Christ says in effect to this father, "Man, the 'if' does not lie with me at all; of course I can heal your son, but you must exercise an expectant faith."

In Matthew 13:58 we read, "And he [Christ] did not many mighty works there because of their unbelief." Unbelief, then, either of the elder or of the sick person, will make it impossible for God to answer prayer. When unbelief kept Christ from healing the sick on earth, it will surely do so today.

In Mark 2:1-5 we have the story of the palsied man who was brought to Christ by four friends and was let down before Him through the roof. In verse 5 we read, "When Jesus saw their faith, he said unto the sick of the palsy, Son, thy sins be forgiven thee." This reads literally, "Jesus, seeing the faith of them" *(autōn),* meaning the faith of the sick man as well as the other four.

But, you ask, "How can we be sure that this pronoun *autōn,* of them or their, includes the sick man as well as the four who carried him?" Because of the pronoun *autōn,* the genitive plural of *autos,* he or himself. If Christ had been here speaking of the faith of these four men only, and not of the sick man, He would have used the demonstrative pronoun *toutōn,* the genitive plural of *houtos,* which would have told us that Christ was referring to the faith "of the persons" nearest to the sick man (the four), but not to the sick man himself.

There are two demonstrative pronouns in Greek; viz., *houtos* and *ekeinos. Houtos,* this one or these, would designate the person or persons nearest to us, while *ekeinos,* that one or those, would designate the person or persons farther away, but neither of these pronouns would include ourselves.

The use of this personal pronoun *autōn,* however, includes the sick man himself and the four others. Yes, "All things are possible to him believing" (Mark 9:23), but without faith on our part, our prayers cannot be answered.

Dealing with this very subject of exercising faith when we pray, James 1:6,7 says, "But let him ask in faith, nothing wavering. For he that wavereth is like a wave of the sea driven with the wind and tossed. For let not that man [who lacks expectant faith] think that he shall receive any thing of the Lord." Then both the elders and the sick persons should have an expectant faith.

Reason VI

Before giving the sixth reason why all God's saints to-day should expect Him to heal their sicknesses, let us here remind you of the five reasons already given.

(1) Because God used to heal the sick as *Jehovah-rapha* (the Lord our Healer), and He is "the same yesterday, and to day, and for ever."

(2) Because Christ died on the cross to atone for our sicknesses, just as He died to atone for our sins.

(3) Because all sickness is the result of Satan's work, when he introduced sin into this world and "Christ was manifested to destroy the works of the devil."

(4) Because the very same Holy Spirit is in the Church today who did all of Christ's miracles and all of Paul's miracles; the very same Holy Spirit who raised Christ from the dead. Since this is true, why should we not expect Him still to heal the sick?

(5) Because of Christ's last Great Commission in Mark 16:15-18, and because of His direct command in James 5:14,15.

(6) And now we come to the sixth and final reason why all true Christians today should expect God to heal their

bodies; viz., because of His marvelous promises, the fulfillment of which depends altogether upon the exercise of our
own faith.

Let us here remind you of some of these promises.
Matthew 18:19, "Again I [Christ] say unto you, That if
two of you shall agree on earth as touching *any thing that
they shall ask, it shall be done for them of my Father* which
is in heaven."

Reader, does "any thing that they shall ask" include
bodily sickness? Yes. Then take Christ as your Healer.

Matthew 21:22, (Christ says), "And all things, whatsoever ye shall ask in prayer, believing, ye shall receive."

Reader, does "all things whatsoever ye shall ask in
prayer, believing" include bodily sickness? Yes. Then take
Christ as your Healer.

Mark 11:22-24, "And Jesus answering saith unto them,
Have faith in God. For verily I say unto you, That whosoever shall say unto this mountain, Be thou removed, and
be thou cast into the sea; *and shall not doubt in his heart,*
but shall believe that those things which he saith shall
come to pass; he shall have whatsoever he saith. *Therefore
I say unto you, What things soever ye desire, when ye
pray, believe that ye receive* [have received] *them, and ye
shall have them."*

Reader, does *"what things soever ye desire, when ye
pray"* include bodily sickness? Yes. Then take Christ as
your Healer.

John 14:13,14, "And whatsoever ye shall ask in my
name, that will I do, that the Father may be glorified in
the Son. If ye shall ask any thing in my name, I will do it."

Reader, does "whatsoever ye shall ask in my name"
and "if ye shall ask any thing in my name" include bodi-

ly sickness? Yes. Then take Christ as your Healer.

John 15:7, "If ye abide in me, and my words abide in you, ye shall ask what ye will, and it shall be done unto you."

Reader, do these words "ye shall ask what ye will" include bodily sickness? Yes. Then take Christ as your Healer.

First John 3:22, "And whatsoever we ask, we receive of him [God], because we keep his commandments, and do those things that are pleasing in his sight."

Reader, does "whatsoever we ask" include bodily sickness? Yes. Then take Christ as your Healer, for He is no "respecter of persons." What He did for John, who made a practice of keeping all His commandments and doing only what was right in His sight, He also will do for you.

James 5:14,15, "Is any sick among you? let him call for the elders of the church; and let them pray over him, anointing him with oil in the name of the Lord: And the prayer of faith shall save the sick, and the Lord shall raise him up; and if he have committed sins, they shall be forgiven him."

Reader, do you believe the Book of James is inspired of God? Yes. Then obey James 5:14 and take Christ as your Healer.

If bodily healing were not in the Atonement — and we have clearly proven it is — we still would have a perfect right to pray for the sick and expect Christ to heal on the authority of the wonderful promises just quoted.

Let us here prove to all our readers that the very same faith that saves the soul also will heal the body.

In Matthew 9:22, Jesus said to the woman with the

issue of blood, "Daughter . . . thy faith hath made thee whole." This expression, "thy faith hath made thee whole," reads in the Greek *Hē pistis sou sesōken se,* and literally reads, "The faith of thee has saved thee." The verb *sesōken* is the perfect tense, 3rd person singular of *sōzō,* I save.

Now examine Luke 7:50. Here Christ says to that poor sinful woman of the street who had anointed His feet with oil and wiped them with the hairs of her head, "Thy faith hath saved thee." This reads in the Greek *Hē pistis sou sesōken se,* and literally reads, "The faith of thee has saved thee." These are the exact same words Christ spoke when He healed the woman with the issue of blood.

Yes, the very same faith which saves the soul heals the body, and this faith is a gift of God, whether for the saving of souls or for the healing of bodies. Ephesians 2:8, "For by grace are ye saved through faith; and that not of yourselves: it [faith] is the gift of God."

We believe all saints ought to expect Christ to heal them until they reach the allotted time of "threescore and ten" years. Many saints are now obtaining wonderful healings even after this age by exercising an expectant faith in God's promises.

And what of those dear saints who suffer year after year and never are healed, although they seem to be utterly yielded to God? All such believe God can heal them, if it is His will, but they lack that expectant faith which says, "I know He will heal me now." They lack this expectant faith simply because they are uncertain as to what His will is concerning them.

Recall here James' words (James 1:7), "For let not that man [who has not expectant faith] think that he shall receive any thing of the Lord." Recall also Christ's own words in Mark 9:23, "If thou canst believe, *all things* are possible to him that believeth." Also Mark 11:24, *"Therefore I say unto you, What things soever ye desire, when ye pray, believe that ye receive them* [have received them], *and ye shall have them."*

Now every Greek scholar must admit that when Christ says, "All things [*panta*] are possible to him believing"(literal translation), and "What things soever [*panta hosa*] ye desire, when ye pray, believe that ye have received them, and ye shall have them," *He puts all responsibility for answered prayer on us, and rolls it off of Himself.* These verses assuredly teach that if we have the expectant faith which God will impart to all who really meet His conditions, there is no sickness He will not cure.

If only we were fully controlled by the Holy Ghost in thought, word, and deed, we would all see miracles performed, both spiritual and physical. Why? Ephesians 3:20, "Now unto him that is able to do exceeding abundantly above all that we ask or think, according to the power [*dunamis,* Holy Ghost power] constantly working [present participle] in us."

Note, God here promises to answer our prayers, "Exceeding abundantly above all that we ask or think, according to the power of the Holy Ghost which is constantly working in us," and not "according to His own will."

Reader, let the Holy Ghost control you in thought, word and deed, and "ye shall ask what ye will, and it shall be done unto you" (John 15:17). Does "what ye will" include your sickness?

Division
II

Division II

Was Divine Healing Only for the Church of the Apostolic Age?

Many Bible teachers today tell us that the age of miracles passed away with the death of the apostles, so Christ is not healing the sick today.

Let us investigate this subject and find out for ourselves.

Listen to Justin Martyr (165 A.D.), one of the great Church leaders and scholars of his day:

He says, "For numberless demoniacs throughout the whole world and in your city, many of our Christian men, exorcising them in the name of Jesus Christ, who was crucified under Pontius Pilate, *have healed, and do heal,* rendering helpless and driving the possessing devils out of the men, though they could not be cured by all the other exorcists, and those who used incantations and drugs" (*Apol. II,* Chapter 6).

Then this Apostolic, miracle-working power was in the Church down to 165 A.D.

Listen to Irenaeus (200 A.D.):

"Those who are in truth His disciples, receiving grace from Him, do in His name perform miracles; and they do truly cast out devils. *Others still heal the sick by laying their hands upon them, and they are made whole.* Yea, moreover, as I have said, *the dead even have been raised up, and remained among us for many years."* (*Vs. Hermetics,* Book I, Chapter 32.)

Then down to 200 A.D. this same Apostolic, miracle-working power was in the Church.

Listen to Origen (250 A.D.):

"And some give evidence of their having received

through their faith a marvelous power by the cures which they perform, invoking no other name over those who need their help than that of the God of all things, and of Jesus, along with a mention of His history. For by these means we too have seen many persons freed from grievous calamities, and from distractions of mind and madness, and countless other ills, which could be cured neither by men or devils" *(Contra Celsum* Book III, Chapter 24).

Then down to 250 A.D. this same Apostolic, miracle-working power was in the Church.

Listen to Clement (275 A.D.):

"Let them (young ministers), therefore with fasting and prayer, make their intercessions, and not with the well arranged, and fitly ordered words of learning, *but as men who have received the gift of healing confidently,* to the glory of God" *(Epis.* C. XII).

Dr. Waterland *(Creation and Redemption,* page 50) says:

"The miraculous gifts continued through the third century, at least." Then he tells how, under Constantine, the Church became flooded with worldliness and began to put its trust in earthly rulers more than in God. But even then those who remained true to God saw miracles performed in His Name.

Theodore of Mopsueste (429 A.D.) says:

"Many heathen amongst us are being healed by Christians from whatever sickness they have, so abundant are miracles in our midst" (Christlieb — *Modern Doubt,* page 321).

Rev. A. Bost *(History of United Brethren,* page 17) quotes the famous Zinzendorf's words, spoken in 1730:

"To believe against hope is the root of the gift of

miracles; and *I owe this testimony to our beloved church, that Apostolic powers are there manifested.* We have had undeniable proofs thereof in the unequivocal discovery of things, persons, and circumstances, which could not humanly have been discovered, in the healing of maladies in themselves incurable, such as cancers, consumptions, when the patient was in the agonies of death, all by means of prayer, or of a single word."

Dr. A. J. Gordon (*Ministry of Healing,* page 65 — a book every saint should read) quotes from the Confession of the Waldenses as follows:

"Therefore, concerning the anointing of the sick, we hold it as an article of faith, and profess sincerely from the heart, that sick persons, when they ask it, may lawfully be anointed with anointing oil by one who joins with them in praying that it may be efficacious to the healing of the body according to the design and end and effect mentioned by the Apostles, and we profess that such an anointing, performed according to the Apostolic design and practice, will be healing and profitable."

No wonder Dr. Gordon says (*Ministry of Healing,* page 43), "Two streams of blessings started from the personal ministry of our Lord, a stream of healing and a stream of regeneration; the one for the recovery of the body, and the other for the recovery of the soul, and these two flowed on side by side through the Apostolic age. Is it quite reasonable to suppose that the purpose of God was that one should run on through the whole dispensation of the Spirit, and that the other should fade away and utterly disappear within a single generation? We think not."

Having now proven that all manner of sicknesses were cured by prayer down to 1750 A.D., the days of Zinzendorf, let us now prove to you that God is still, today, healing all manner of diseases in answer to the prayer of faith.

Modern Miracles of Healing

(1)Violet M. Collins, Vancouver, B.C., was born without a rectum passage. Best surgeons in Toronto operated. Told she could not live. Was anointed and prayed for, and instantly made as normal as any other girl.

(2) Mrs. H. R. Shortreed, Vancouver, B.C., had sugar diabetes in advanced stage. Anointed, prayed for and healed.

(3) Mrs. Jean C. Barker, West Vancouver, B.C., and Mrs. M. M. Meadows, Vancouver, B.C., both had operations for dreadful cancers. Mrs. Barker had both breasts removed. These cancers grew again. Both women anointed and prayed for; today are well.

(4) B. M. Colwell, Vancouver, B.C., was cured by prayer of dreadful stammering, an affliction from boyhood. This was a marvelous healing.

(5) Reuben Mark Scotcher, Vancouver, B.C., had "adhesions of the bowels" for nine years. Operated on, but became much worse. Also ruptured. Anointed, prayed for and healed by the Lord Jesus. Mr. Scotcher is a Presbyterian elder.

(6) Mrs. Frances McClurg, Vancouver, B.C., was paralyzed 19 years, and her eyesight almost gone. Was anointed, prayed for, and healed completely by the power of God. She threads the finest needle today.

(7) Mrs. Zeva Parker, Oklahoma City, Oklahoma, known as "Dare Devil French Bobby," jumped from a plane two thousand feet high at the Fair Grounds. The parachute failed to open until she was almost down. Her back was broken in three places and seven ribs were so

fractured that they protruded through the flesh. She was rushed to the hospital and put in a plaster of paris cast. Doctors said she would never walk. She was instantly healed while lying on her cot in Dr. C. S. Price's meeting. She had been converted, but had not as yet been prayed for. She has since won many souls to Christ by her wonderful testimony.

(8) Miss Ruby Dimmick, daughter of Rev. J. F. Dimmick of Albany, Oregon, was paralyzed as a child. One leg was left two inches shorter than the other and that limb had not developed as the other. While she was sitting in the Metropolitan Church, Victoria, B.C., at Dr. Price's meeting, God suddenly touched her. Her leg extended, developed as the other limb, and was instantaneously cured. That was in 1923, and her limb is well today. Note, she, too, had not yet been prayed for.

(9) Miss Bertha Irvine, Lebanon, Oregon, had been an invalid 19 years. After four operations she was not able to stand on her feet without support. She was anointed and prayed for, then the evangelist cried, "Sister, in the Name of Jesus of Nazareth, rise up and walk." She arose immediately and ran up and down the aisle. The writer was present when both Miss Dimmick and Miss Irvine were healed by the power of God. Miss Irvine was cured in November 1922 and is well today.

(10) Reginald Williams, West Vancouver, B.C., cut off the top part of his left thumb at the joint below the nail. He was anointed and prayed for, and God caused that part to grow on again, nail and all. Examine both thumbs and you cannot now tell on which one God performed this wonderful miracle.

Reader, what God has done for these sick saints He

is ready to do for you. Read again the promises quoted on pages 46-49, then drop on your knees and claim your healing on the authority of these promises and the fact that the Lord Jesus Christ died for your sickness as well as for your sins.

The writer can vouch for every case here given, and knows of scores of others who have had just as wonderful cures as these mentioned. Most of the cases here recorded are taken from the Miracle Number of *Golden Grain*, December 1929.

The writer, while investigating this subject, secured the names and addresses of the 800 persons prayed for in one campaign. A year later he got in touch with all these by personal visitation and by sending out "return postcards," and found that more than 60 percent had been healed, and most of those who were not healed said they had received a great spiritual blessing. They confessed that they had a "hope so faith," rather than a "know so faith."

Just here we desire to say that fully one-half of these 800 who were prayed for had troubles which their physicians counted either incurable or very hard to be cured.

Division
III

Division III

Objections Answered

I. If we are to expect God to heal the sick today through prayer, why not also expect Him to raise the dead?

Because we are nowhere commissioned to raise the dead, although Irenaeus asserts (as quoted before) that the dead were raised in his day (200 A.D.).

In Mark 16:17,18 we read, "And these signs shall follow them that believe . . . they shall lay hands on the sick, and they shall recover."

Again James 5:14,15 says, "Is any sick among you? let him call for the elders of the church; and let them pray over him, anointing him with oil in the name of the Lord: And the prayer of faith shall save the sick, and the Lord shall raise him up." *Note, God has not here told us to raise the dead, but only to pray for the sick.*

II. If healing is in the Atonement and some saints are not healed, then these saints must conclude that they are still sinners in God's sight and under His condemnation, no matter how close to God they are living.

This is the great objection of many splendid Bible teachers to healing in the Atonement.

Let Paul answer this objection. He says (1 Cor. 11:29), "For he that eateth and drinketh unworthily, eateth and drinketh damnation [*krima*, judgment] to himself alone [*eauto*, reflexive pronoun], not discerning the Lord's body."

The word for "discerning" here is *diakrinōn*, the present participle of *diakrinō*, and means "making a distinction between." What distinction is here referred to? Read First Corinthians 11:30, "For this cause [because you do not discern between the significance of the bread and the wine when partaking of the Sacrament] many are weak

and sickly among you, and many sleep [are prematurely
dead]."

Paul here asserts that many Christians are weak and
sickly and others have died prematurely because they had
partaken of the Sacrament without understanding — as
they ought to have understood — the great distinction between the significance of the bread and the wine. What
is this distinction?

In Exodus 12:7 we read that the Israelites put the blood
of that first Passover lamb on their door posts to save
themselves from the wrath of God, but Exodus 12:8 informs us that God commanded them to cook the flesh of
the first Passover lamb and eat it for their own physical
benefits.

Now read First Corinthians 5:7, "For even Christ our
passover is sacrificed for us." If Christ is our Passover
lamb, His blood was most assuredly shed to save us from
the wrath of God through the forgiveness of our sins, and
His flesh was bruised and broken for our physical benefits.
"By the bruise of whom ye were healed physically" (1 Peter
2:24, literal translation).

Remember that this word "healed" *(iaomai)* without
one exception in the New Testament refers only and
always to physical healing, never to spiritual healing. This
is positive proof to all Greek scholars that Peter is here
speaking of our "physical healing" through the awful suffering of Christ. See pages 25-28 for the true exposition
of First Peter 2:24.

First Corinthians 6:19,20, as we have clearly proven,
teaches this very same truth, that Christ died to redeem
our bodies as well as our souls. First Corinthians 6:19,20,
"What? know ye not that your body is the temple of the

Holy Ghost which is in you, which ye have of God, and ye are not your own? For ye are bought [redeemed] with a price: therefore glorify God in your body, and in your spirit, which are God's."

Note, our bodies and our spirits have been redeemed with the very same price; viz., the blood of Christ. See pages 28-33 for the true exposition of First Corinthians 6:19,20.

Although the blood of Christ, our Passover lamb, was shed to save us from the wrath of God, and His body was bruised and broken for our physical benefits, the failure of any saint to discern this distinction, when partaking of the Sacrament, does not make that saint guilty in the sight of God. Read again First Corinthians 11:29, "For he that eateth and drinketh unworthily, eateth and drinketh damnation [*krima*, judgment] to himself alone [*eautō*, reflexive pronoun], not discerning the Lord's body."

If, when partaking of the Sacrament, we fail to discern the true significance of the bread because of ignorance or wrong teaching, we bring judgment upon ourselves alone in that we must continue sick or die prematurely, but it does not affect, in any way, our standing in God's sight. This is the exact meaning here of the reflexive pronoun *(eautō)*. As Paul declares in Romans 8:1, "There is therefore now no condemnation [*katakrima*, sentence standing against] to them who are in Christ Jesus."

Yes, healing, is in the Atonement, but no saint is held guilty in God's sight who fails for any reason to discern this fact; he only suffers himself.

III. If healing is in the Atonement, then every saint has a blood-bought right to be healed; and yet all saints are not healed.

One Bible teacher says, "We must add, that if it were true that Christ died for our sicknesses, then His atoning work in this respect is a failure . . . The choicest saints on earth today are the thousands of shut-ins, who suffer in patience and sing their sweet songs in the night." (*The Healing Question,* pages 74,75.)

Reader, did Christ die to save all sinners? Yes, you reply. Then every sinner in this world has a blood-bought right to be saved? Yes. But are all sinners saved? No, only a very small percentage. Then, according to the writer just quoted, Christ's atoning work in this respect also is a tremendous failure.

Why are not all sinners saved, since they have a blood-bought right to be saved? Because they refuse to meet God's conditions as set forth in John 1:12,13; John 3:16,18,36; John 5:24; and Romans 10:9,10.

It is just the same with bodily healing. *Every saint has a blood-bought right to be healed, but thousands do not know that they must exercise the very same appropriating faith in the bruised body of Christ for their healing as they formerly exercised in His shed blood for their salvation.*

In Luke 7:50, Christ says to a poor sinful woman, as we stated before, "Thy faith hath saved thee." The word here for "hath saved" is *sesōken,* the perfect, 3rd singular of *sōzō,* I save. In Luke 8:48, Christ says to the poor woman who had an issue of blood twelve years, "Thy faith hath made thee whole." The word here for "hath made thee whole" is this same word, *sesōken,* the perfect, 3rd singular of *sōzō,* I save. This, then, is positive proof that the very same faith that saves the soul also will heal the body. Many saints do not understand this because of ignorance or false teaching, and therefore they are not healed.

What Conditions Must Saints Meet To Be Healed
(1) *We must make an absolute surrender to God: a 100 percent consecration. This is what John did, and all his prayers were answered.* First John 3:22, "Whatsoever we ask, we receive of him, because we keep his commandments, and do those things that are pleasing in his sight." John made a practice of keeping all of God's commandments and doing only what was right in His sight, and the result was that God answered all his prayers. Now God is no respecter of persons.

(2) *Our hearts must be pure.* Psalm 66:18, "If I regard iniquity in my heart, the Lord will not hear me." Remember, God sees what men cannot see.

(3) *We must realize that our bodies belong to God,* and that every organ, without exception, must be used in a way well pleasing to Him and for His glory, not for our own selfish or sensual pleasure. Read First Corinthians 6:19,20 and Romans 12:1.

(4) *We must exercise a genuine expectant faith in the promises of God.*

(NOTE: God demands of us that we have faith. Without faith it is impossible to please Him (Heb. 11:6). If God demands that we have faith when it is impossible for us to have faith, then we have a right to challenge His justice. But if He places within our hands the means whereby faith can be produced, then the responsibility rests with us whether we have faith. He has provided the way whereby everyone can have faith — and He has told us exactly how to get faith. "So then faith cometh by hearing, and hearing by the word of God" (Rom. 10:17). Faith grows out of the Word of God. Meditate on the Word. Dig deeply into it and feed upon it. What natural food is to

the physical man, the Word of God is to the spiritual man.
It is faith food. It produces faith. There is really no other
way to secure faith. — Kenneth E. Hagin)

**IV. Hundreds of preachers and Bible teachers today
object to divine healing because of James 5:14,15:**

"Is any sick among you? let him call for the elders of
the church; and let them pray over him, anointing him with
oil in the name of the Lord: And the prayer of faith shall
save the sick, and the Lord shall raise him up; and if he
have committed sins, they shall be forgiven him."

These persons object to the elders of the church obeying this command today for two reasons:

(1) They hold the Epistle of James is not for this Church
Age at all, but for the twelve tribes scattered abroad, or,
as others teach, for the Jews of the Tribulation Period.

(2) Because the Greek word *aleipsantes*, having
anointed, really means "having massaged," or "having
smeared" with oil the one to be prayed for — thus using
oil as a remedy — and does not mean to simply touch with
oil the surface of the skin as all do today when praying
for the sick. Such a use of oil, all these objections tell us,
would demand the word *chrio* and not *aleipho*, the word
used in James 5:14.

Let us here give five great scriptural reasons why we
know James is for this Church Age and not alone for the
twelve tribes scattered abroad or for the Jews of the
Tribulation Period.

(1) The use of the words "My beloved brethren" prove
for a certainty that the Epistle of James is for this Church
Age. James uses this term three times. James 1:16, "Do
not err, my beloved [*agapētoi*] brethren." James 1:19,
"Wherefore, my beloved [*agapētoi*] brethren." James 2:5,

"Hearken, my beloved [*agapētoi*] brethren."

Paul uses these words only when referring to Church saints. First Corinthians 15:58, "Therefore, my beloved [*agapētoi*] brethren, be ye steadfast," etc. Philippians 4:1, "My brethren, dearly beloved [*agapētoi*] and longed for, my joy and my crown," etc.

This word *agapētoi*, as all true Greek scholars must admit, always, without one exception in the New Testament, refers to the Church saints, as in First John 3:2, "Beloved [*agapētoi*], now are we the sons of God,"etc.

In Greek there are different words for love. *Phileo* means to love as a friend; *stergo,* to love in the sense of being fond of; but the strong word is *agapaō*, which is always used of God's love. (See John 3:16.) All through the New Testament, the love expressed by this verb *agapaō*, or by the noun *agapē,* or by the adjective *agapētoi,* always refers to God's own love, or to the love which God's Holy Spirit has created in man's heart.

Then whenever you find the expression "beloved" (agapētoi), or "my beloved brethren" (adelphoi mou agapētoi), these expressions always, without one exception, refer to the Church saints.

Now, as we have shown, James uses these expressions three times. Therefore, we know for an absolute certainty that the Book of James is for the Church saints today. Any other conclusion is only unscholarly nonsense which reveals a lamentable ignorance of Greek; especially in the light of Galatians 3:28, where we are told that in the Church "There is neither Jew nor Greek, there is neither bond nor free, there is neither male nor female: for ye are all one in Christ Jesus."

From this expression "My beloved [*agapētoi*]

brethren," we know that these twelve tribes scattered abroad must have been Christian Jews and therefore members of Christ's Church. This being so, then this epistle is just as much for us Gentiles as for them. Why? Ephesians 2:14, "For he [Christ] is our peace, who hath made both [Jew and Gentile] one, and hath broken down the middle wall of partition between us."

(2) Again we know the Epistle of James is for this Church Age, because James himself so declares.

James 5:14, "Is any sick among you? let him call for the elders of the church [*ekklēsia*]."

We recently heard a much-advertised Bible teacher declare in Seattle that the word "church" here in James 5:14 ought to read "synagogue" *(sunagōgē)*. This is utterly absurd, because James says, "Call for the elders of the church [*ekklēsia*]." Now this word *ekklēsia* means Church and comes from *ek,* out of, and *kaleo,* I call — those called out of the world to worship Christ. Now who constitutes the Church *(ekklēsia)?* Read Acts 2:47, "And the Lord added to the church daily such as should be saved." Then every saved person, whether of the twelve scattered tribes or of the Gentiles, was a member of the *ekklēsia* (Church) in James' day, so what James wrote for the Church then is for Christ's Church today. Any other conclusion is only unscholarly nonsense.

Reader, when James says (James 5:14), "Is any sick among you? let him call [imperative mood] for the elders of the church [*ekklēsia*]," why pay any attention to the opponents of divine healing whose minds are so distorted by bitter prejudice that they deny James was here writing to the Church *(ekklēsia),* but only to Jews who were not Church members?

We had better believe James' own words (James 5:14) and act as Paul advises us to act under such circumstances. Romans 3:3,4, "For what if some did not believe? shall their unbelief make the faith of God without effect? God forbid: yea, let God be true, but every man a liar."

(3) Again we are absolutely sure this epistle is for this Church Age, because James uses the expression *en eschatais hēmerais* (in the last days). James 5:3, "Ye have heaped treasure together for the last days."

As these words are used elsewhere in the New Testament, we can discover the exact time to which James here refers.

In Acts 2:17 Peter says, "And it shall come to pass in the last days [*en tais eschatais hēmerais*], saith the Lord, I will pour out of my Spirit upon all flesh," etc. Then, according to Peter, "the last days" is a time when the Holy Spirit will be here, for He is then to be poured out upon all flesh. When, therefore, James says (James 5:30), "Ye have heaped treasure together for the last days," he is speaking of a time when the Holy Ghost will be here, so most assuredly it is referring to this Church Age just before Christ's Second Coming and not to the time of the Tribulation, when the Holy Ghost will have gone up with the Church. See Second Thessalonians 2:7,8.

In Second Timothy 3:1-4 we read, "This know also, that in the last days [*en eschatais hēmerais*] perilous times shall come. For men shall be lovers of their own selves, covetous, boasters, proud, blasphemers, disobedient to parents," etc.

Now all who believe in the Second Coming of Christ quote these words to prove that we are now "in the last days," according to Paul's vivid description, and James says (5:3), "Ye have heaped treasure together for the last days." As James here uses the very same words as Paul in Second Timothy 3:1; viz., *en eschatais hēmerais* (in the last days), we can only conclude that he is speaking of the very same time as Paul, the time just before the Lord Jesus returns for His saints.

In Second Peter 3:3,4 we read, "Knowing this first, that there shall come in the last days scoffers, walking after their own lusts, And saying, Where is the promise of his coming [*parousia*]?" Here the expression "the last days" refers to the very same time as Second Timothy 3:1; viz., the time just before the *parousia*, or the coming of Christ for His saints. Then most assuredly when James says (5:3), "Ye have heaped treasure together for the last days," he, too, refers to the time just before the Lord's return for His saints. Thus again we are absolutely sure this epistle is for all the saints of this Church Age and not for the Jews of the Tribulation Period, or the twelve scattered tribes of James' own day.

(4) Again James 5:7,8 affords us positive proof that this epistle is for this Church Age. James 5:7,8, "Be patient therefore, brethren, unto the coming [*parousia*] of the Lord ... Be ye also patient; stablish your hearts: for the coming [*parousia*] of the Lord draweth nigh."

If this "coming of the Lord" *(parousia)* which James speaks of is the coming of Christ for His saints, then most assuredly James is writing his epistle for all the saints of this Church Age.

Let us examine this coming of the Lord, which James here designates the *parousia*, a word which literally means "being with" or "presence."

Speaking of the different resurrections, Paul says (1 Cor. 15:23), "But every man in his own order: Christ the firstfruits; afterward they that are Christ's at his coming [*parousia*]." Here all Bible students admit that Paul is speaking of Christ's coming for His saints.

First Thessalonians 4:15-17 makes this very clear, "For this we say unto you by the word of the Lord, that we which are alive and remain unto the coming [*parousia*] of the Lord shall not prevent [go before] them which are asleep. For the Lord himself shall descend from heaven with a shout, with the voice of the archangel, and with the trump of God: and the dead in Christ shall rise first: then we which are alive and remain shall be caught up together with them in the clouds to meet the Lord in the air: and so shall we [the saints] ever be with the Lord."

Then the dead saints are to rise and be caught up with living saints at the *parousia.*

Having now proven conclusively that the *parousia* is the coming of Christ for His Church saints, let us again read James 5:7,8, "Be patient therefore, brethren, unto the coming [*parousia*] of the Lord . . . Be ye also patient . . . for the coming [*parousia*] of the Lord draweth nigh."

The inevitable and only conclusion that unprejudiced minds can possibly draw from these words is that James wrote for all the Church saints, both Jews and Gentiles, for he urges them to be ready for the *parousia,* which is the coming of Christ for His Church saints.

To sum up: We have now given four irrefutable reasons why we can be sure that the Epistle of James is for the saints of this Church Age.

(1) Because the words "My beloved [*agapētoi*] brethren" used by James are only employed in the New Testament to designate the Church saints and no one else.

(2) Because James declares himself that he is writing

to the Church saints. James 5:14, "Is any sick among you? let him call for the elders of the church [*ekklēsia*]," etc.

(3) Because James is writing to a people living "in the last days" *(en eschatais hēmerais),* an expression referring to this Church Age just before the Second Coming of our Lord.

(4) Because James urges the people to whom he writes to remember that the *parousia* (the coming of Christ for His Church) draweth nigh.

(5) *But there is a fifth great reason why all Greek scholars know, for a certainty, that the Epistle of James is for this Church Age. James asserts that the Holy Spirit was even then abiding in the persons to whom he wrote.*

James 4:5, "Do ye think that the scripture saith in vain, The spirit that dwelleth in us lusteth to envy?" Literally this reads, "The Spirit which took up His abode in us," or "the Spirit which moved into us to abide" *(katōkēsen).* The use of this verb *katōkēsen,* the 1st Aorist, 3rd singular of *katoikeo,* I take up my abode, proves conclusively that James is here speaking of the Holy Spirit, and not of the man's own spirit.

This forces us to the conclusion that James wrote his epistle for a people into whom the Holy Spirit had come to abide, and to abide, as we have seen, till the *parousia,* when Christ comes for His Church.

In the face of these five reasons, what must we think of the Greek scholarship of Bible teachers and pastors who tell us that the Epistle of James is not for this Church Age?

We do not want to be unkind, but we will declare most emphatically, in the light of the five reasons just given, that no Bible teacher or preacher — unless blinded by prejudice — will ever say the Epistle of James is not for this

Church Age but those who are either utterly ignorant of Greek, or have such an imperfect knowledge of this wonderful language that it is useless to them in expounding the Word of God.

Since the Epistle of James is for this Church Age, until the *parousia* (the coming of our Lord), and since James 5:14,15 refers to physical sickness, had we not better obey Christ's command here (James 5:14,15)? "Is any sick among you? let him call for the elders of the church; and let them pray over him, anointing him with oil in the name of the Lord: And the prayer of faith shall [not probably will] save the sick, and the Lord shall raise him up."

Anointing with Oil

Objectors to divine healing today tell us that the Greek word for "anointing" (*aleipsantes,* having anointed) in James 5:14 always means "to massage, to smear, or to daub" the whole body, or some certain part of the body, as when Christ's feet were anointed (Luke 7:38).

These objectors tell us there is not one place in Greek literature where this word *aleipho* does not mean "to massage, smear, or daub," and this is positive proof that God means the oil in James 5:14 to be used as a remedy for sickness. They conclude, therefore, that James 5:14 teaches us not only to pray for the sick, but to use healing remedies as well. This is a serious objection if true, so let us make a thorough investigation.

Let us here read James 5:15 and see if the "anointing with oil" plays any part in curing the sick. James 5:15, "And the prayer of faith shall save the sick [not the anointing with oil], and the Lord shall raise him up." "The anointing with oil," then, was to play no part whatsoever in curing the sick; only the prayer of faith could do this.

What, then, is the significance of the anointing with oil in James 5:14?

The Greek word is *aleipsantes,* the 1st Aorist participle of *aleipho,* I anoint, and therefore literally reads "having anointed."

It is only fair here to state that this word *aleipho* does mean "to massage, to plaster (Ezekiel 13:10,11 in *Septuagint*) and to daub" (Ezekiel 22:28 in *Septuagint*), but this word is used in another sense, which all opponents of divine healing have overlooked, or more likely never have seen.

Let us here examine Exodus 40:13 and 15 in the *Septuagint* (the version Christ used more than any other), and we will see clearly the scriptural explanation of anointing with oil in James 5:14.

In Exodus 40:13, God says to Moses, "And thou shalt put on Aaron the holy garments, and thou shalt anoint [*chriseis*] him, and thou shalt sanctify him," etc.

Then in Exodus 40:14,15, God says to Moses, "And thou shalt bring up his [Aaron's] sons, and shalt put garments on them. And thou shalt anoint [*aleipseis*] them, as thou didst anoint their father," etc.

The word "as" here is the Greek expression *hon tropon,* and literally means "which manner." This expression emphatically declared that Moses must anoint Aaron's sons in the very same manner that he anointed Aaron himself.

Consult Babbitt's *Greek Grammar,* page 186, or any other good Greek grammar, and you will find that *tropon,* the accusative of *tropos,* is often used in this adverbial sense, as in Acts 1:11, ". . . this same Jesus, which is taken up from you into heaven, shall so come *in like manner as* [*hon tropon*] ye have seen him go into heaven."

But why does God employ the word *chrio* (I anoint by touching the surface of the skin) when anointing Aaron, and the word *aleipho* when anointing Aaron's sons, *though He commands Moses to anoint both father and sons in the very same manner?* By the use of these two different words, God desired to let us know that, in His sight, there was a great difference between Aaron and his sons.

What was this difference? Let me here quote from C. H. M.'s *Notes on Leviticus,* page 20: "If Aaron was a type of Christ, then Aaron's house was a type of Christ's house, as we read in Hebrews 3, 'But Christ as a Son over His own house: whose house we are.' And again, 'Behold, I and the children whom God hath given me.' "

Since Aaron was a type of Christ, our great High Priest, God employs the same word *(chrio)* to express his anointing with the Holy Ghost (Luke 4:18). But Aaron's sons were only a type of Christ's Church. "His house," or the children whom God had given Christ; therefore, their anointing is expressed by the less sublime word *(aleipho).* *But remember that Aaron's sons were anointed in the very same manner as Aaron himself, by simply touching the surface of the skin, though a different word is used to express this anointing; viz., aleipho, the very word we find in James 5:14.*

Here, then, we have the true scriptural explanation of this word *aleipsantes,* having anointed, in James 5:14. When we today anoint a sick saint with oil by touching the surface of the skin, as Aaron's sons were anointed in Exodus 40:15, we recognize the blessed fact that this person has been regenerated and belongs to the Church, the household of Christ, our great High Priest, and therefore has a perfect right to claim all the benefits of Christ's redeeming love.

Division
IV

Division IV

Why Are So Many True Saints of God Not Healed?

(1) *Many saints are not healed because of false teaching.*
They have been taught that sickness and pain are sent by God Himself to chasten them and make them wholly submissive to His will. Hebrews 12:6, "For whom the Lord loveth he chasteneth, and scourgeth every son whom he receiveth."

These dear saints pray for patience to be submissive to God's will, who has (as they suppose) so severely afflicted them, and yet they at once send for a physician and a nurse and begin to take medicine or have an operation in order to get rid of this disagreeable experience, which, they believe, God has brought upon them to beautify their character. Is this submission to God's will if one really believes that this sickness has been sent of God? No!

These saints cannot pray the prayer of faith to be healed, because they believe it is God's will that they should be sick, but they can, with no compunction of conscience, send for a physician and use all possible human remedies to get rid of that which God has sent upon them for their good. Human nature is indeed a funny thing.

Just here recall Christ's words (Matt. 9:12), "They that be whole need not a physician, but they that are sick." This is true. Every sick person does need a physician, and if he or she, for any reason, cannot exercise expectant faith in the promises of Christ, the Great Physician, then all such should send for a doctor. Praise God for the many noble physicians in our land who go forth day or night, in good or bad weather, to relieve suffering. Many often drive miles to serve poor people, though they know they

will not receive a dollar. Among our physicians today are
many noble men of God who believe in prayer, and always
ask God's help before they prescribe or perform an
operation.

May God bless the noble doctors of our land, and no
exponent of divine healing should ever say or write an
unkind word against them.

If Christian people are sick, and for any reason cannot meet God's conditions for imparting to them expectant faith, then let them get a physician, and the sooner
the better.

*Many splendid Christians are not healed by prayer,
because they cannot pray the prayer of expectant faith.*
They say, "Perhaps God does not desire to heal me yet,"
and this "perhaps" causes a doubt in their heart. James
says (James 1:7), "Let not that man [who has any doubt
in his heart] think that he shall receive any thing of the
Lord."

All such saints should read First Thessalonians 4:3,
"For this is the will of God, even your sanctification."

(2) *Other saints are not healed because they always ask
with the proviso "if it be thy will."*

We cannot blame them, for they read in such books as
The Healing Question, pages 127-128, "The most essen-
tial element in believing prayer is to ask according to His
will. It does not say, 'If we ask anything according to our
will He heareth us,' but 'If we ask anything according to
His will, He heareth us' (1 John 5:14). Without this, prayer
is not real prayer, nor real faith, but dictation to God,
which must be more obnoxious to Him than when a child
comes to an earthly father and insists on having that which
the father knows would only hurt his child. The highest

prayer which lips of clay can pray is the prayer the Son
of God prayed in dark Gethsemane, 'Nevertheless not my
will but thy will be done.' And thus the child of God prays
still, and such a prayer is acceptable and well pleasing in
His sight.'' (See note III, Addenda Notes.)

With such false teaching so prevalent today, no wonder
the majority of saints know little or nothing regarding
divine healing.

In First John 5:14,15, we read, "And this is the confidence that we have in him, that, if we ask any thing according to his will, he heareth us: And if we know that
he hear us, whatsoever we ask, we know that we have the
petitions that we desired of him."

Who wrote these words? John. But John wrote (John
15:7), "If ye abide in me, and my words abide in you, ye
shall ask what ye will, and it shall be done unto you."

Note, John here declares that, under certain conditions,
we can ask according to our own will, and our prayers will
be answered.

John also tells us that he himself got from God
whatever he asked for, and tells us how we can do the
same. First John 3:22, "And whatsoever we ask, we receive
of him, because we keep his commandments, and do those
things that are pleasing in his sight."

When the opponents of divine healing quote First John
5:14 so frequently, why do they never quote John 15:7;
First John 3:22; and Matthew 15:21-28? In Matthew
15:21-28, Christ tests to the very limit the faith of that
Syrophenician mother who brought her demon-possessed
daughter to Him, and then He says to her, "O woman,
great is thy faith: be it unto thee even as thou wilt. And
her daughter was made whole from that very hour."

The only reason these opponents of divine healing do not quote these passages is because they prove their teaching regarding prayer to be absolutely false, and they are too prejudiced against divine healing to face the truth of God squarely.

Andrew Murray truly says, "It simply is impossible to pray with faith when we are not sure that we are asking according to the will of God. As long as one prays thus, inserting the proviso, 'if it be thy will,' one is praying with submission but this is not the prayer of faith."

Then no one can possibly pray the prayer of faith which saves the sick (James 5:15) and put in the proviso "if it be thy will."

When we pray for a very sick person and ask God to heal him, if it be His will, we virtually say, "Lord, I do not know whether You desire to heal this person or let him die, but whatever You do, Lord, will please me, so do not let my request to have him live make any difference to You whatsoever." Such a prayer as this reveals fatalism, not faith.

In Mark 11:22-24, we read, "Have faith in God. For verily I say unto you, That whosoever shall say unto this mountain, Be thou removed, and be thou cast into the sea; and shall not doubt in his heart, but shall believe that those things which he saith shall come to pass; he shall have whatsoever he saith. Therefore I say unto you, What things soever ye desire, when ye pray, believe that ye receive [*elabete,* have received] them, and ye shall have them."

Note the words "and shall not doubt in his heart." To pray the prayer of faith, Christ says, we must ask and not doubt in our hearts. Now no one can possibly pray this prayer of faith unless he knows for a certainty that it is God's will to heal the one being prayed for. When we inject the proviso "if it be thy will," it is always an acknowledgment that we are not praying the prayer of faith, but that we have a doubt in our own heart; and James says (James 1:7), "Let not that man [who prays with a doubt in his heart] think that he shall receive anything from the Lord."

Yes, when we pray the prayer of faith for healing, we must believe that we have already received that for which we have prayed, and have no doubt about this fact (Mark 11:22-24). But such a prayer cannot possibly be offered unless we know it is God's will to heal.

Here is a sinner you are trying to lead to Christ. He asks you, "Does not God now know whether I will be saved or lost?" "Yes," you reply. Then he says, "Well, if I am going to be saved, I will be saved, and if I am going to be lost, I will be lost, so it is all up to God. I have no responsibility in the matter."

You would call this fatalism, not faith, and you would explain to him that to be saved he must meet God's conditions for salvation. Just so, beloved, when you pray for the sick and insert the proviso "if it be thy will," you are placing all the responsibility of that healing on God and assuming absolutely none yourself. You forget that Christ has set down certain hard and fast conditions which must be met before He will answer prayer.

Read Matthew 21:22, "And all things, whatsoever ye shall ask in prayer, believing, ye shall receive." Insert "if it be thy will," and you cannot ask "believing," for you put all responsibility then on God and assume none yourself.

In Mark 9:22, the father of a demon-possessed boy says to Jesus, "If thou canst do any thing, have compassion on us, and help us." Christ replies (Mark 9:23), "If thou canst believe, all things are possible to him that believeth." Then that father cries out, "Lord, I believe; help thou mine unbelief," and Christ immediately cured his son. Christ let him know that the "if" (the responsibility of the cure) did not lie with Him, but with the father himself. How some people forget this.

Again read Mark 11:22-24, and see how God puts all responsibility for answered prayer on us. He says here, as plainly as language can express it, that answered prayer does not depend upon His will at all, for it is always His will to answer the prayers of any of His children who will meet the one and only condition of expectant faith. Think now as you read:

Mark 11:22-24, "And Jesus answering saith unto them, Have faith in God. For verily I say unto you, That whosoever shall say unto this mountain [both a literal mountain, or a mountain of sickness], Be thou removed, and be thou cast into the sea; and shall not doubt in his heart, but shall believe that those things which he saith shall come to pass; he shall have whatsoever he saith. Therefore I say unto you, What things soever [this includes all sicknesses] ye desire, when ye pray, believe that ye receive [literally, have received] them, and ye shall have them."

If certain scholars are right in saying we should always, when we pray, insert the proviso "if it be thy will," why did Christ say to the two blind men (Matt. 9:29), "According to your faith be it unto you"? Why did He not say, "According to my will be it unto you"? *Because God has placed the responsibility for answered prayer on us and not upon Himself.* Mark 9:23, "Jesus said unto him [the father of the demon-possessed boy], If thou canst believe, all things are possible to him that believeth."

Here compare two passages of Scripture: (1) First John 5:14, "This is the confidence that we have in him, that, if we ask any thing according to his will, he heareth us." (2) Ephesians 3:20, "Now unto him that is able to do exceeding abundantly above all that we ask or think, according to the power [*dunamis*, Holy Ghost power] constantly working [present participle] in us."

John asserts that God answers prayer "according to [kata] his will." Paul asserts that God answers our prayers and gives us far more than we ask "according to [kata] the Holy Ghost power constantly working in us." How do we reconcile these assertions? Romans 8:27 gives the explanation, "And he that searcheth the hearts knoweth what is the mind of the Spirit, because the Spirit maketh intercession for the saints according to God" (*kata theon*, literal reading).

This simply means that it is possible for God's saints to be so controlled by the Holy Ghost in thought, word, and deed that He will control all their prayers, making these harmonize with God's will. John was so controlled, so he says (1 John 3:22), "Whatsoever we ask, we receive of him, because we keep his commandments, and do those things that are pleasing in his sight." Oh, that God would inspire every saint to follow John's example!

Yes, beloved, God has specified certain conditions which we must meet before He "wills" to answer our prayers, but if we refuse to meet these conditions and put all responsibility on Him by inserting "if it be thy will," our prayers will never be answered.

There is a proper time and place to insert "if it be thy will" when we pray. Read James 4:13-15: "Go to now, ye that say, To day or to morrow we will go into such a city, and continue there a year, and buy and sell, and get gain: Whereas ye know not what shall be on the morrow . . . For that ye ought to say, If the Lord will, we shall live, and do this, or that."

If we are thinking of changing our place of abode and yet are not certain that this change is pleasing to God, we ought to say, "Lord, I would like to move to this other city and do this or that, but perhaps thou dost want me to remain here. Master, I want only to do thy will, so if thou wouldst have me remain here, reveal this fact to me in some way."

This is the only thing to do when we are uncertain of God's will.

Reader, if it were ever God's will that any of His saints should remain sick, would He have given us that great command in James 5:14,15? "Is any sick among you? let him call for the elders of the church; and let them pray over him, anointing him with oil in the name of the Lord: And the prayer of faith shall save the sick [physically sick, as we have proven], and the Lord shall raise him up."

Note the word "let him call for" *(proskalesasthō).* This is the 1st Aorist, imperative, middle of *proskaleo,* I call. In the middle voice this word means "to call or summon for one's own benefit or aid." The Aorist imperative demands immediate action. It demands that the command be executed and be made a past event at once.

Here, then, we have a direct command from God Himself that every saint, when sick, should at once call to his aid the elders of the Church, and just as direct a command (imperative, Aorist) that the elders should pray over the sick person, having first anointed him with oil in the Name of the Lord.

Now some of us are fully persuaded that, if it were ever God's will that His saints should remain sick, in place of here saying, "And the prayer of faith shall save the sick, and the Lord shall raise him up," James 5:15 would have read, "And the prayer of faith shall [if it be God's will] save the sick, and the Lord shall [if it be His will] raise him up." Since God did not here insert this proviso when giving us this gracious command, why should we insert it?

Remember John 15:7 says, "If ye abide in me, and my words abide in you, ye shall ask what ye will, and it shall be done unto you." Note, Christ here asserts that if we abide in Him and His words abide in us, we can then ask whatever we will, and it shall be done unto us.

Then under certain conditions, Christ here declares, we can all have whatever we will when we pray, and we do not need to insert the proviso "if it be thy will."

Division
V

Division V

1. Some Closing Remarks

In closing, we desire to declare, on the authority of God's Word, that there is bodily healing for every saint who will meet the conditions for answered prayer, because Christ died for our sicknesses just as He died for our sins. (See pages 10-35.)

All who deny that healing is in the Atonement forget the words of Peter. First Peter 2:24, " . . . by whose stripes [bruise] ye were healed [*iathēte*]." This Greek word *iathēte* (ye were healed) is the 1st Aorist passive, 2nd person plural of the deponent verb *iaomai*, a word that always in the New Testament refers to physical healing.

But why is the Aorist tense used here, "By whose bruise ye *were* healed"? The Aorist is here used for the very same reason that it is used in Romans 5:6, "For when we were yet without strength, in due time Christ died [*apethanen*] for the ungodly." Here the Aorist tense, *apethanen* (2nd Aorist, 3rd singular of *apothnēsko*, I die), brings out the great truth that Christ died once for all to save sinners. We see the same truth brought out by the Aorist tense in First Corinthians 15:3, " . . . Christ died [*apethanen*] for our sins according to the scriptures." *Apethanen*, died, is 2nd Aorist, 3rd singular of *apothnēsko*, I die, and brings out the thought of something fully completed in the past. We see this same great truth, that Christ died once for all for our sins, in Revelation 5:9, " . . . for thou wast slain [*esphagēs* — 2nd Aorist of *sphazō*, I slay], and hast redeemed [*egorasas*, 1st Aorist of *agorazo*] us to God by thy blood."

In all these cases, the use of the Aorist tense brings out the great truth that when Christ died for our sins, He died once for all: His redemptive work was then completed forever. Now this is the exact meaning of the Aorist in First Peter 2:24, ". . . by whose bruise ye were physically healed [*iathēte*]."

The use of the Aorist tense in Romans 5:6, First Corinthians 15:3, Revelation 5:9, and elsewhere where Christ's redemptive work is spoken of proves that He has now made it possible for every sinner to be saved who will meet the needful conditions. And the use of the Aorist tense *(iathēte)* in First Peter 2:24 proves that by His redemptive work He has, in the very same way, made it possible for every sick person to be healed who will meet the needful conditions for praying the prayer of faith.

Yes, the use of the Aorist tense iathēte (ye were physically healed) in First Peter 2:24 expresses the glorious truth that Christ has made the very same provision to heal our body as to save our soul.

Here recall Christ's own words again:

Matthew 21:22, "And all things, whatsoever ye shall ask in prayer, believing, ye shall receive." Reader, does "all things, whatsoever" include your sickness? Yes.

Mark 9:23, "Jesus said unto him [the father of the demon-possessed boy], If thou canst believe, all things are possible to him that believeth." Reader, does "all things" here include your sickness? Yes.

Mark 11:24, "Therefore I say unto you, What things soever ye desire, when ye pray, believe that ye receive [or have received] them, and ye shall have them." Reader, do these words "What things soever ye desire, when ye pray" include your sickness? Yes.

John 15:7, "If ye abide in me, and my words abide in you, ye shall ask what ye will, and it shall be done unto you."

Reader, do these words "Ye shall ask what ye will, and it shall be done unto you" include your sickness? Most assuredly, if only you will meet the conditions laid down. When you do meet these conditions of John 15:7, and the Holy Ghost is controlling you in thought, word and deed, a spirit of praise, thanksgiving, and joy will dominate you. "The joy of the Lord" will then be your strength.

Praise God, His promises are sure, and He is able to meet our every need.

2. A Startling Question

Why is it that far more souls today are being won to Christ by the evangelists who believe that James 5:14 is a command of God to be obeyed by all saints than by any other evangelists? This is a startling fact.

In one three-week campaign where the sick were being anointed and prayed for, the writer saw from 500 to 1,000 souls coming to God night after night. In one meeting, in a Chinese theater, the evangelist preached to 900 heathen Chinese through an interpreter, and 400 of them came to God and were wonderfully saved. The Holy Ghost was there with tremendous convicting power. Then followed the most remarkable healing service we have ever witnessed. Blind eyes were opened; deaf ears were unstopped; goiters melted away; and all kinds of diseases were healed by the mighty power of God.

The interpreter's wife, who had been brought in on a stretcher dying of tuberculosis, was anointed and prayed for and was completely healed. She is perfectly well today after seven years.

Many splendid Bible teachers and preachers are today bitterly opposing all evangelists who "anoint with oil" and

pray for the sick in public, as Christ and His disciples used
to do.

Christ preached and healed in public. See Matthew
8:16; Matthew 9:35; and Mark 1 and 2. All Christ's
miracles were wrought in public. Christ told His disciples
to preach and heal in public (Matt. 10:6-8). Christ commanded "the Seventy" to preach and heal in public (Luke
10:1-12). Peter and John healed in public (Acts 3:6-11). Paul
preached and healed in public (Rom. 15:18,19).

Can you find anything in the Word forbidding men to
preach and pray for the sick in public? No. Then let us
be careful how we criticize these servants of God, for Bible
teachers and evangelists who have bitterly opposed this
movement have become harsh and have lost their soul-
winning power. They seem to have grieved the Holy Ghost.

*Yes, each of these much-maligned evangelists who
prays publicly for the sick is today winning far more souls
to God each year than all his opponents combined.*

Soul-winning, remember, is not the work of man, but
of God; so when God is thus blessing these evangelists
who pray for the sick according to James 5:14, we are
forced to the conclusion that these are the men most
honored by the blessed Holy Spirit, because they are living nearest to the center of God's will and are obeying His
Word as other evangelists are not.

Ephesians 3:20, "Now unto him that is able to do exceeding abundantly above all that we ask or think, according to the power [*dunamis*, Holy Ghost power] that is constantly working in us [exact meaning here of present par-
ticiple]," etc.

Reader, to what extent is the Holy Spirit constantly
working in you? The answer to this question will deter-

mine the measure of your usefulness to God. Remember, it is written (Zech. 4:6), "Not by might, nor by power, but by my spirit, saith the Lord of hosts."

Addenda Notes

I. From page 19. This is exactly what we should expect, for Mark 16:20 declares that after Christ ascended to heaven and sat on the right hand of God, the disciples went forth and preached everywhere, the Lord constantly working in conjunction with them *(sunergountos)*, and confirming His Word with signs following. This is the exact translation of *sunergountos*, the present participle, genitive, of *sunergeo* (I work in conjunction with).

Since Mark here emphatically asserts that Christ, after He had ascended to God's right hand, did still continue to constantly work in conjunction with His disciples (the exact meaning here of the present participle), and so caused miracles to happen, why should we not believe him?

II. From page 32. Listen to Ephesians 1:14, "Which [the Spirit] is the earnest of our inheritance until the redemption [*apolutrōsis*] of the purchased possession." Paul here declares that we have already been purchased, the price for our redemption has been paid, but we are not yet free from the consequences of our former sinful state. This complete and final future freedom Paul here terms our *apolutrōsis*.

III. From page 81. Was Christ in any doubt concerning God's will when He said in the garden, "Nevertheless not my will, but thine be done"? No! He knew that He had come to this world as God's sinless Lamb to die for man's sin.

In the following passages He declares over and over again that He must die and rise again the third day. See Matthew 20:18 and 19; Mark 8:31, 9:31, and 10:34; Luke 18:32 and 33, 24:45 and 46; and John 2:19-22 and 6:51. These passages, together with Acts 2:23, prove that Christ well knew it was the Father's will that He should die on

the cross. When, however, He faced the awful agony of
that Roman flogging and the physical suffering of the
crucifixion, His human nature revolted, and, seeing this,
Satan urged Him not to carry out His Father's will.
Remember, Christ was tempted in all points "like as we
are, yet without sin" (Heb. 4:15). By the power of the Holy
Ghost, He conquered Satan and cried out, "Not my will,
but thine be done," but He well knew it was God's will
that He should die.

In the face of this fact, it is perfectly absurd to teach
that all Christians today should pray, as Christ prayed
in the garden, "Nevertheless not my will, but thine be
done." He never had a doubt regarding God's will.

When Bible teachers assert that all true prayer must
include the proviso, "if it be thy will," what will such
teachers do with God's own declaration in Isaiah 45:11?
"For thus saith the Lord God, the Holy One of Israel . . .
enquire of me concerning my sons, and concerning the
works of my hands command me" *(Septuagint)*.

Is man the work of God's hands? Yes. Then God here
says, "Concerning the works of my hands command me"?
One thing is certain, Isaiah 45:11 can never mean anything
to the timid saint who always prays with the proviso "if
it be thy will." Such persons will never even desire suffi-
cient faith to act as God commands all His saints to act
in Isaiah 45:11.